D0480139

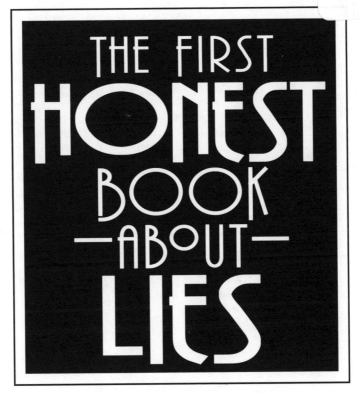

THE FIRST HONEST BOOK ABOUT LIES

JONNI KINCHER

Edited by Pamela Espeland

Free Spirit
PUBLISHING

Copyright © 1992 by Jonni L. Kincher

All rights reserved. Unless otherwise noted, no part of this book may be reproduced in any form, except for brief reviews, without written permission of the publisher.

Kincher, Jonni, 1949–
    The first honest book about lies / Jonni Kincher.
        p.   cm.
    Includes bibliographical references and index.
    Summary: Readers learn how to discern the truth from lies through a series of activities, games, and experiments.
        ISBN 0-915793-43-1
    1. Truthfulness and falsehood—Juvenile literature. 2. Deception—Juvenile literature. [1. Honesty.] I. Title.
    BF637.T77K56   1992
    155.9'2—dc20   92-13403
                                                                         CIP
                                                                          AC

Cover and book design by MacLean and Tuminelly
Index compiled by Eileen Quam and Theresa Wolner

10 9 8 7 6 5 4 3
Printed in the United States of America

FREE SPIRIT PUBLISHING INC.
400 First Avenue North, Suite 616
Minneapolis, MN 55401
(612) 338-2068

"A Christmas Memory" on page 69 is used with permission of Dan Barnhart, professional actor and musician. The "Five Family Myths" on pages 99-101 are used with permission of Becky Blanchard, Andrea Groener, Kristin Jacobsen, Marcus Koch, and Mary-Ann Sontag for Nikki Sontag. "Finding Your Truth" on page 151 is used with permission of Philip Higgins.

This book is dedicated to my three sons, Adam, Joe, and Travis:

In hopes that each of you may first and always remain true to the only person you can ever honestly know: yourself.

Dear Reader,

Elbert Hubbard once said, "The best service a book can render you is not to impart truth, but to make you think it out for yourself."

This is what I hope this book can do.

ACKNOWLEDGMENTS

I would like to acknowledge the great research assistance and help with the Bibliography which Adam Kincher gave me so generously.

CONTENTS

Chapter 8
All Hat and No Cattle 121
Public relations and media lies

Chapter 9
You Are an Agent of Truth 137
How to live in a world of lies

INTRODUCTION

True or false?
Columbus discovered America.

When you answer a true/false question, you have a clear and simple choice. You choose your answer, and it's right or wrong.

Right...or wrong?

Consider the Columbus question. Some people would answer TRUE—that Columbus did discover America. Others would answer FALSE—that America was already here, that Native Americans had already "discovered" it, or that someone else—perhaps Leif Ericson?—discovered it long before Columbus.

If life were as simple as a true-or-false test, you wouldn't need to weigh the truth. You wouldn't need to question what you hear, read, and learn in school. You wouldn't need to think for yourself.

But life isn't simple, and you simply can't believe all of the information that is served up to you. You have to ask questions. Not just any questions, but the right questions. And you must insist on answers. Not just any answers, but answers that really mean something.

Before you can look for the truth, you must first find out what the truth means to you. One person's truth is another person's lie. You might say, "Tomatoes are delicious," and that would be true for you. But it wouldn't be true for someone who hates tomatoes. The only way to determine what is and isn't true for you is to become aware of the world and your own way of looking at it.

Here's where *The First Honest Book about Lies* comes in. It can help you discover your truth. Each chapter invites you to look at lies in a fair and balanced way, without telling you what to think.

As you read, first notice the different kinds of lies, then really think about them. How are they used on you, around you, and by you? What purposes do they serve—or are they always self-serving?

"Each reader reads only what is already inside himself. A book is only a sort of optical instrument which the writer offers to let the reader discover in himself what he would not have found without the aid of the book."

—Marcel Proust

I

Try the activities, games, and experiments. What do they reveal about how you feel about each type of lie, and about lies in general?

Hop on this interesting and sometimes maddening roller-coaster ride through half-truths, fibs, and outright falsehoods you hear every day but may not be aware of. Soar to see the lies your own senses tell you. Dip down to the past and uncover some history "facts" which began as fabrications. Do the loop-the-loop as you learn that made-up myths can reveal great truths. At the end of the ride, you'll be a living lie detector—knowledgeable, aware, and able to scope out the truth wherever it lies.

Once you learn the truth about lies, you're on your own to decide how much you want to live within the truth you find. Sometimes living within the truth means doing without, looking funny, being lonely, or missing opportunities.

These decisions are up to you, because *The First Honest Book about Lies* can't tell you how to live your life. No book can do that. If this book pretended to tell you how to live...to never lie, to always put other people first...well, it just wouldn't be an honest book.

The only "how to live" suggestions you'll find on these pages are labeled "TRUTH #__." These are observations most people eventually learn from experience.

TRUTH #1:
IF YOU LEND A BOOK,
CHANCES ARE YOU'LL NEVER GET IT BACK.

If this book can't tell you how to live, what can it do for you? It can help you become a wiser consumer, a more thoughtful and responsible citizen, and a better friend to yourself and others. It can give you a clearer picture of your personal standards for honesty and truth. It can change the way you see your world—and that's the truth.

Jonni Kincher

CHAPTER 1

TRUTH IS STRANGER THAN FICTION

The final statement on the back cover of this book is true.

"YES, VIRGINIA, THERE IS A SANTA CLAUS"

In 1897, a little girl named Virginia became so upset when her friends told her there was no Santa Claus that she wrote a letter to a newspaper to discover the truth. The newspaper printed a reply from Frances P. Church in which he wrote, "Yes, Virginia, there is a Santa Claus."

This phrase is now part of our cultural language. We usually understand it to mean that something can be true in spirit or feeling even if it isn't true in fact.

In a famous movie from 1939, another little girl named Dorothy discovered that the Wizard of Oz was a fake. She called him "a very bad man" for pretending to be a real wizard.

YES, VIRGINIA, THERE IS
A SANTA CLAUS

This editorial, which first appeared in *The New York Sun* on September 21, 1897, has been reprinted thousands of times throughout the world.

Dear Editor:

I am eight years old. Some of my little friends say there is no Santa Claus. Papa says, "If you see it in The Sun it's so." Please tell me the truth. Is there a Santa Claus?

> *VIRGINIA O'HANLON,*
> *115 W. 95th St.*

Virginia, your little friends are wrong. They have been affected by the skepticism of a skeptical age. They do not believe except they see. They think nothing can be which is not comprehensible by their little minds....

Yes, Virginia, there is a Santa Claus. He exists, as certainly as love and generosity and devotion exist, and you know that they abound and give to your life its highest beauty and joy. Alas, how dreary would be the world if there were no Santa Claus! It would be as dreary as if there were no Virginias. There would be no childlike faith then, no poetry, no romance, to make tolerable this existence. We should have no enjoyment except in sense and sight. The eternal light with which childhood fills the world would be extinguished....

No Santa Claus! Thank God, he lives, and he lives forever. A thousand years from now, he will continue to make glad the heart of childhood.

> FRANCIS P. CHURCH

Both Virginia and Dorothy may have felt, "Maybe you just can't trust anybody anymore." But when Mr. Church wrote, "Yes, Virginia, there is a Santa Claus," and the Wizard replied, "I am a very good man, just a very bad wizard," they were being typical grown-ups. Many adults try to make life pleasant for children. They want the world to be a magical place for them. At the same time, most adults realize that their children will be unhappy if they don't learn to deal with life as it really is.

The painful truth is that adults can't make life perfect. Even when they are very good people, they are very bad wizards.

Think back to the first time you learned that someone you trusted was lying to you. How did you feel? How did you react? Were you upset and confused like Virginia? Disappointed and angry like Dorothy? Did you blame the other person for lying? Or did you blame yourself for believing the lie?

Did you laugh the whole thing off? Or did you take it as proof that nobody could be trusted? Did you follow up to find out the whole truth or the reason for the lie?

Some people insist on absolute honesty at all times. They would rather hear and speak the truth, even when it's brutal. Other people would rather not hear the truth about some things. Still others are the "Yes-Virginia-there-is-a-Santa-Claus" type. They spend more time weighing lies than condemning them.

When it comes to honesty vs. lies, where do you weigh in?

> **"Sorry, Virginia, I'm sure you're a nice little girl, but your future depends on you, not on believing in Santa Claus."**
>
> —Andy Rooney

WHERE DO YOU WEIGH IN?

To begin to get an idea of where you weigh in on the truth, consider the following cases and rate each one on the Lie Line.

If you're shocked, give the case a 10. If it's no big deal, give it a 0. If it falls somewhere in between, rate it somewhere in between.

---

0   **10**

LIE LINE

Case #1: Newspaper columnist William Safire "confessed" in one of his columns that his first résumé misrepresented his experience.

In that résumé, he described himself as being "as familiar with the streets of New York as with the streets of Paris." In fact, he had never been to either city. Technically, his statement was true.

Most job-seekers soon discover that "you can't get a job without experience, and you can't get experience without a job." Even basically honest people have been known to stretch the truth on job applications and résumés.

Was Safire's statement an outrageous lie or a realistic solution to a common problem?

Case #2: Many students feel they have too much reading to do. So instead of tackling the real classics (like *Moby Dick* and *A Tale of Two Cities*), they read much shorter versions published by Cliff's Notes or Monarch Notes. This lightens their study load.

Are these students cheating their teachers, or just cheating themselves out of a learning experience? Are they lying or using their time wisely?

Case #3: Many United States holidays including Memorial Day, Veterans' Day, and Presidents' Day are not celebrated on the same calendar day each year. They are moved to Mondays to create three-day weekends.

Does this give us more time to pay our respects? Or is it just an excuse to take another day off? Do you think this practice is basically dishonest, or do you think it doesn't matter?

TRUST: THE FIRST STAGE

However you react to lies, your feelings of trust or mistrust were probably formed when you were an infant.

Psychologist Erik Erikson mapped out eight stages of human development, with each stage presenting a specific situation or "life crisis" to solve. He called the first stage *trust vs. mistrust.*

As an infant, you needed food, warmth, cuddling, and sleep to survive. Because you were helpless, you had to rely on others to meet your basic needs. If most of your needs were met during this first important stage, you learned to trust people and to view the world as a safe and satisfying place.

But what if your first year of life was filled with people who wouldn't or couldn't meet your needs, or who met your needs angrily? You learned to mistrust people and to see the world as a frustrating, even threatening place.

LIES YOU HAVE KNOWN

1. What is the biggest lie…
   a) you have ever been told?
   b) you have ever told someone else?

2. What is the first lie you remember…
   a) someone telling you?
   b) telling someone?

3. What is the best (kindest) lie...
   a) you have been told?
   b) you told someone else?

4. What is the worst (meanest) lie...
   a) you have been told?
   b) you told someone else?

5. What is the most transparent (obvious) lie...
   a) you have been told?
   b) you told someone else?

6. What is the most believable lie...
   a) you have been told?
   b) you told someone else?

Trust is important to everyone's well-being. Basic trust gives you the courage to speak your truth. No wonder Virginia was shocked to find out that the people she trusted had let her believe in a Santa Claus who isn't real! No wonder Dorothy was hurt when she learned that the "wonderful Wizard" was only human! Discoveries like these divide people.

Not only is it more difficult to *speak* your truth after someone you trust has lied to you, it's also more difficult to *hear* the truth after that. To return to your former level of trust, you must decide that you really weren't betrayed after all; that the deception was harmless, or even kind. You must also figure out where the lie fits in with your own system of values and your own standard of what is acceptable.

It takes two for the truth to be known: one to speak it, and one to hear it. Sometimes the hearer has the harder job.

SANTA STUDIES

Most children stop believing in Santa Claus between ages six and eight. Studies show that they are relieved to give up the pretense. Most parents, however, go on believing that their children still believe in the jolly old elf.

Cornell University psychologist John Condry surveyed 500 children in first through sixth grades and their parents. He found that parents often said that their children still believed in Santa, but

"I stopped believing in Santa Claus when I was six. Mother took me to see him in a department store and he asked for my autograph."

—Child star Shirley Temple

the children themselves would say, "I gave that up a year ago." By this time, the children were lying to their parents! They didn't want to disappoint their parents by letting them know that they no longer accepted the Santa story. Interestingly, girls were more likely than boys to pretend to still believe in Santa. They were afraid that the gifts might stop coming if they admitted to knowing the truth. Also, they felt that their parents expected them to believe.

Condry's study further showed that while many parents felt guilty about the Santa lie, their children didn't resent them for it. Maybe Virginia wasn't really worried about Santa's existence after all. Maybe the letter was her way of telling her parents that she knew the truth.

" 'Tis strange—but true; for truth is always strange, stranger than fiction."

—Lord Byron

"Truth is stranger than fiction—to some people."

—Mark Twain

BECOMING A LIVING LIE DETECTOR

It isn't always other people who lie to you. Sometimes your own assumptions and perceptions lead you astray. You follow self-deception down many alleys which the truth would never enter. Your feelings and behaviors become confused.

As you learn about truth and lies, you become a living "lie detector," sensing when the truth is being twisted to influence your feelings and behaviors. You start asking questions to help you decide if there's enough evidence to meet your standard for truth.

For example, you've heard the statement, "All Irish people like the color green." You might ask yourself, "How do I know this is true?" Your evidence might be, "I once saw an Irish person wearing green." But is that enough for you?

The power source for your inner lie detector is *knowledge*. The more you know about everything—especially about the many methods used to influence you—the more you can see and hear the truth.

The scale which weighs the evidence is your own clear, simple thinking, which separates opinions from facts. Instead of thinking in simple "true-false" terms, your lie-detecting self says, "This would seem to be true (or not) based on the evidence available to me."

Your honest look at lies robs them of their power. The only way lies can cause trouble for you is by disguising themselves as the truth.

YES, VIRGINIA, THERE WAS AN UNCLE SAM

Most people assume that Uncle Sam, a symbol of the United States, is a made-up character.

In fact, he was a real person. And believe it or not, he was a boyhood friend of Johnny Appleseed (real name: John Chapman), another American legend who turns out to be real.

Uncle Sam was born Sam Wilson. During the War of 1812, he supplied meat to troops stationed around Troy, New York. The meat was stamped "U.S." for "United States."

Once, when a government inspector came to check the meat, he was told by a worker in Wilson's store that "U.S." stood for "Uncle Sam"—Sam Wilson's nickname.

In the early 1960's, the U.S. Congress officially proclaimed Sam Wilson as the original Uncle Sam. But Sam Wilson didn't wear the tall hat and striped pants you've seen in drawings of Uncle Sam. And he didn't have a long white beard.

BIG LIES, LITTLE LIES

Big lies tend to STOMP in loudly and announce themselves in flashing neon letters: "I AM A LIE." This is why big lies may be less important than the small lies which merely (tiptoe) into your daily life.

You know the big lies are there. It's the small lies that can shape your thinking and actions without your sensing their presence or influence.

Small lies can add up to big, sneaky lies which hide themselves within an invisible web of deceptions. But when you look at them closely, those deceptions unravel quickly to expose the lies and drain them of their power.

When you think you are getting twice as much because there is "50% more," when you believe a new shampoo will make you irresistible, when you choose a friend who flatters you—and then make decisions based on these beliefs—you may not be acting in your own best interests. Lies can hurt you when you don't see them for what they are. This is why you need to know the truth about lies. So take an honest look.

"It is not disbelief that is dangerous to our society; it is belief."

—George Bernard Shaw

TRUTH IS STRANGER THAN FICTION

CHAPTER 2

SNIFFING OUT THE TRUTH

Complete the following sentence:
A zebra is a horse-like animal which is _____ (color) with _____ (color) stripes.

CAN YOU BELIEVE YOUR EYES?

One morning, a patient of psychiatrist Oliver Sacks experienced a miracle. He awoke to the smell of coffee and could even smell his pipe.

Why was this a miracle? Because the man had no sense of smell. He had lost it as the result of a head injury. The smells of coffee and his pipe were all in his mind, recreated from memory.

Some people have been known to feel pain in amputated limbs. Others have reported seeing pools of water in the desert.

It's true: Your own senses can lie to you. Only part of what you smell, taste, feel, hear, and see is based on what is really out there in the world. The rest is created by your memory and imagination.

When you picture a zebra in your mind, is it a black animal with white stripes? Or a white animal with black stripes? People from countries of mostly dark-skinned people tend to see a black animal with white stripes. But those from countries of mostly light-skinned people tend to see a white animal with black stripes.

Different people see the same reality in different ways. Their truth depends on their perception and judgment.

How you view a zebra is unlikely to influence your attitudes, decisions, or daily living. Sometimes, however, the meanings people place on reality cause disagreements large enough to start wars.

Is the truth a black animal with white stripes, a man with no ability to smell, a painful leg, and pools in the desert? Is the truth a white animal with black stripes, the smell of coffee and pipe tobacco, a missing leg, and no pools in the desert? Or is the truth some combination of these realities?

If you can't believe your senses, what can you believe?

SENSE STATISTICS

- You may wonder whether a zebra is white-on-black, or black-on-white. To the tsetse fly, that question is irrelevant. Scientists have found that the zebra's black-and-white striped coloring makes it virtually invisible to the pesky tsetse. For the fly, zebras are "nonexistent."

- The brain of a cat has the ability to see in color, but cats normally see in black-and-white.

- High-frequency sounds make the skin more sensitive.

- A small African fox called a fennec can hear movements of another animal up to one mile away.

- A baby's cry happens to be at the pitch our hearing is most sensitive to.

- People living in more primitive environments tend to have the best-developed senses. The Bushmen of Africa's Kalahari Desert can hear approaching airplanes from 70 miles away.

- Women have keener senses than men. This isn't a sexist statement; just a fascinating fact to be found (with many others) in Marc McCutcheson's book, *The Compass in Your Nose and Other Astonishing Facts about Humans.*

PERCEPTION AND SENSATION

Philosophers needed to know the answer to the basic question, "What IS the truth?" They thought they might find some clues if they took a look at the causes behind illusions.

Meanwhile, physiologists wanted to know why our senses fool us. They wondered how information obtained by the senses could be perceived differently by different people, or perceived wrongly. They asked, "Why are there illusions?"

When philosophers and physiologists got together to investigate these matters, a new field of study called *psychology* was born. In 1879, a man named Wilhelm Wundt started a laboratory in Leipzig, Germany to study human perception. His laboratory is thought to be the place where scientific psychology began.

The study of perception eventually led to modern psychology, which includes the study of behavior, learning, social interaction, language, and, more recently, artificial intelligence.

Psychologists soon found that perception and sensation are not the same. Your senses bring information to your brain from the outside world. This information is in the form of *sensations*. Then your brain goes to work and organizes the sensations, using your past experience and present knowledge so the sensations will make sense to your view of reality. This organization of sensations is called *perception*.

Or, to put it simply: Your senses bring in meaningless signals, which your brain changes into meaningful information.

If you and a two-month old infant look at a poster with the letters D-O-G written on it, both of you have the same sensation. The same pattern of light and dark hits your retinas. However, when your brain processes this information, you have a totally different perception of the poster than the infant has.

The infant has no awareness of words or language. Your past experience (you have learned to read) gives you the perception of D-O-G as a word which stands for an animal. The infant has little or no experience with dogs. Your emotions enhance your perception as you visualize a certain kind of dog (collie, Doberman) or maybe even a particular dog (Benji, Rover).

SENSATION VS. PERCEPTION

Sensation

Sensation is input.

Look at the image. Lines, shapes, and shades hit your retina as signals are sent to your brain. The image makes an impression on your visual receptors. You don't need any learning or experience to receive this impression.

This is *sensation.*

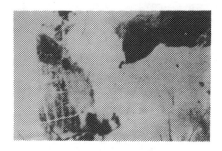

WHAT IS THIS?

Perception

Perception is organization of input.

Look at the image until you can identify it as a "cow." The organized lines, shapes, and shades which cause you to conclude that you "see" a cow make up your *perception.*

Your ability to perceive the picture as a cow depends on your past experience and present knowledge. You must have some idea what a cow looks like, even if you've never seen one in real life.

To get an even more striking picture of how the brain organizes identical sensations into unlike perceptions, compare the perceptions of people from different environments and cultures.

When you were a child, you may have thought that an airplane left the ground, grew smaller, and eventually disappeared. But you have learned from your environment and culture that when large objects are far away, they only look small.

When you stand on a ridge and look out on a field where cattle are grazing, you view them as normal-size cattle which happen to be far away from you. This is a judgment you make, not what you actually see. Your sensation—the image hitting your retina—is one of tiny animals. But your perception is a distant herd of cattle.

Now imagine that you are standing on that same ridge with a boy who has never seen a horizon before. How do you think he will perceive the same herd of cattle? Probably as a herd of ants! He has learned from his environment and culture that objects which appear tiny are tiny. When you live in an environment where you never see objects at great distances, your visual field is different, and your focus is closer.

Is it any wonder nations get into situations where each is absolutely sure that truth and right are on their side?

TRUTH AND ILLUSION

Your truth is the result of your expectations, past experiences, feelings, logic, and intellect, plus the smells, sights, sounds, flavors, and textures that surround you. But *your* truth isn't necessarily THE truth.

To know THE truth, you must have *all* the facts and *all* the possible points of view. This makes finding THE truth out of the question. But you can sniff out the truth if you discover the reasons behind illusions, and apply these reasons to other areas of your life.

Information is the bridge between *your* truth and THE truth. Without enough information, or with the wrong kind of information, THE truth remains illusive. As you acquire more and better information, *your* truth moves closer to THE truth.

"Don't part with your illusions. When they are gone, you may still exist but you have ceased to live."

—Mark Twain

1. **Some illusions are based on incomplete information.** Would more information change *your* truth or bring you closer to THE truth? Would it help you to make more sense of the situation?

2. **Some illusions are based on conflicting information.** Are people around you sending you mixed messages? How about "get good grades" vs. "it isn't cool to study"? Can you choose the message that's best for you by taking a long-term view? Which one would make you better off tomorrow, next week, or next year?

3. **Some illusions are based on misleading information.** Be aware of who and what may be trying to influence you (peer pressure, advertising, etc.). Are you basing your decisions on what's best for *you*? Or are you basing them on what other people are doing and saying?

4. Some illusions are based on unrealistic expectations. Are you expecting too much or too little of yourself or others? Do your expectations match up with real possibilities and probabilities? Do you raise your expectations so high that you are often disappointed?

5. Some illusions are based on false or exaggerated comparisons. Is it *disastrous* to miss the party, or just unfortunate? Can you really compare your life with someone else's, considering all the different factors involved? Are you feeling unnecessarily bad or unrealistically good because you're comparing yourself to other people?

AMBIGUOUS FIGURES

Ambiguous figures are illusions caused by equal cues telling you to identify a particular object as a rabbit *and* a duck, an old woman *and* a young girl. The information on both sides is so balanced, and the evidence is so convincing, that you end up with two true answers to the question: "What is this a picture of?" It's like hearing two sides of the same story, then deciding which one to believe.

There are many areas of life where true/false, either/or won't get you any closer to the truth. Sometimes there really *can* be two opposites which both seem to be true, at least until additional information is available to you.

The *figure/ground illusion* is a specific type of ambiguous figure. At first, you can't determine which part is the object and which part is background. Are the stairs going up or down? Are you seeing a white vase on a black background, or shadowed profiles on a white background?

This is a variation of the equal cues problem, with special meaning for life situations. Being able to tell the figure from the ground is like pulling the essence of truth from what you read or hear.

Some things aren't totally true, but they have a "grain of truth" in them. If you can train yourself to separate the relevant and true information from the "background"—the extra, distracting information—you will take a giant leap toward detecting the truth.

This will be very useful whenever people try to mislead you by drowning out meaningful words with a lot of meaningless words. The real information is the "figure," and the meaningless words are the "background."

The image you see in an ambiguous figure depends on where you focus. For example, focus on the "beak" in the

duck/rabbit illusion and you tend to see a duck. Focus on the
"nose" of the rabbit and the rabbit appears. Focus on the white
center area of the vase/faces and you see a vase. Focus on the
profiled chins and you see two faces.

WHAT DO YOU SEE?

An ambiguous figure can be seen in different ways. Your brain
receives cues from the image that tell you to identify it as one
thing, and an equal number of cues that tell you to identify it as
something else.

1. Old woman or
young woman?

2. Duck or rabbit?

3. At least 5 ways
to see this!

4. Stairs up or down?

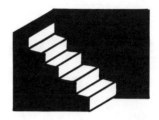

5. Faces or vase?

INTERPRETING THE FIGURES

Figure 1: Why do you think some people more easily see the old woman, while others see the young woman? Experiment by showing the figure to older and younger people, and to males and females. Can you find a pattern in their responses? (If you're still having trouble seeing one figure or the other, the nose of the old woman forms the cheek and chin of the young one.)

Figure 2: If you say, "That's a duck," and the next person says, "That's a rabbit," who is telling the truth? Adding information will change the picture. Sketch in whiskers, and the figure is clearly a rabbit; color the beak (ears?) orange and it's a duck. Often, a little more information is all you need to reach an agreement about what constitutes the "truth."

Figure 3: What you see in this figure depends on where you focus and what you expect to see. There is a star; three blocks in various positions; a mask-like face with diamond eyes; etc. Is your vision limited, or are you able to see life situations in many different ways?

Figure 4: Stare at the stairs and they will appear to flip-flop! Did you ever suddenly see something in your life in a new and different way?

Figure 5: Do you see a white vase? Or two shadow profiles facing each other? This figure contains the same amount of visual cues for each. What do you do when you have equally good reasons for doing two different things, and you can't do both? Do you study for the history final, or attend your grandmother's 100th birthday bash? Go to the beach, or go to the mountains?

AGREEING TO DISAGREE: A MATTER OF FOCUS

How we see the truth may depend on where we focus. Imagine that you overhear four people arguing about whether their country should get involved in a war.

1. Helen is *against* the war because "if we go to war, hundreds of thousands of lives will be lost, including those of innocent women and children."

2. Paul is *for* the war because "it puts people to work in the defense industry, and that's good for the economy."

3. Ned is *against* the war because "millions, maybe billions of dollars will be spent—and for what?"

4. Jennifer is *for* the war because "lives may be saved by stopping a tyrant before things get out of hand."

When Helen and Jennifer debate the issues, they both focus on the *human life* aspect of war, even though one is for it and the other is against it. When Paul and Ned argue, they both focus on the *economic* aspect of war, even though one is for it and the other is against it.

What happens when Helen (against war/lives will be lost) argues with Paul (for war/good for the economy)? Or Ned (against war/too costly) argues with Jennifer (for war/lives may be saved)? Each has a completely different focus. They are unlikely to resolve their debate. They may not even agree to disagree.

Here are a few truth-seeking questions to ask yourself in cases like these:

- Is one person looking at the short-term and the other at the long-term?

- Is there another difference in focus besides the most obvious one(s)?

- Is the truth hidden in the background while you are focusing on the foreground? Or is the truth right there in the foreground while you are focusing on the background?

- Is it sometimes more important just to find a *common* ground?

FOCUS IN

When you focus on the foreground, a double image is always present in the background. You ignore this unusual state of affairs. But when you focus on the background, you see a single image.

Have you ever noticed that the background seems fuzzy when you're not focusing on it? When you watch a movie, the background is unclear, but you usually just ignore it.

FOCUS-IN EXPERIMENT

Look at an object across the room against a plain background. Hold your finger in front of you at arm's length so you can see the object and your finger at the same time.

Focus on your finger and notice the background at the same time. Your target object in the background will appear as a double image.

Now put the object in focus, and you'll see it as a single image.

Finally, focus on the object, continuing to notice your finger. What do you see? Two fingers—until you focus on your finger again.

THE BAD OLD "GOOD OLD DAYS"

Are you tired of hearing about the "good old days" when politicians were honest, schools were excellent, drug problems were nonexistent, the environment was clean, people were caring, the poor were few, and families sat around the fireside together reading great literature? You may wonder why things are so much worse today.

The lie is that "everything in the past was better than it is now." The truth is that "some things probably were better then, but some were surely worse."

History, like the good old days of your own childhood, tends to grow sweeter over time. Events look different when you look back at them than when they occurred. The lens of time may place them out of focus.

To avoid being fooled, don't accept that the past was the way people say it was. Scan old newspapers and magazines to see for yourself. You'll probably find an article from the 1930's telling of the decadence of youth, the terrible state of education, and so forth. It might be fun to copy the article, remove the date, and see if others can guess when it was written.

Contemporary sources—those written at the time events really happened—give a more accurate view of what people were doing and thinking than sources written long afterward. Our own "current events" will look very different in history books written 100 years from now.

Here are a few truths about the good old days that may surprise you:

- Between 1860 and 1890, it's estimated that the crime rate in the United States rose more than twice as fast as the population.

- In 1868, a newspaper article stated, "Each day we see ghastly records of crime...murder seems to have run riot and each citizen asks...'Who is safe?'"

- In the late 1860's, there were a hundred thousand drug addicts in America. (This figure doesn't include people addicted to alcohol, which wasn't considered a drug in those days.)

- Poverty was so bad that half the population of New York City lived in slums. In the late 1800's, the city had clogged sewers, garbage everywhere, and pigs running freely in the streets.

- Early death was so common in the 1800's that there were proportionally the same number of single-parent families in the United States then as there are today.

So much for the good old days!

Putting history in focus will keep you from being taken in by the "single-demon fallacy." You may have heard people say things like, "THE problem is high taxes," or "If it weren't for the drug problem, things would be the way they used to be." Beware of these simple-sounding, one-size-fits-all appraisals of life. There is seldom *one* problem, *one* solution, or a perfect past to return to.

COMPARED TO WHAT?

Sometimes you can determine the truth by taking a new look at an accepted "standard."

For example, the standard size of doorways in the United States is about 6'8" high x 2'6" wide. You rarely encounter a doorway much larger or smaller than this.

When movie directors want an average-size actor to look like a larger-than-life hero, they put him in a smaller-than-normal doorway. Audiences see him on the big screen and think, "Wow! That guy must be almost 6 feet 8 inches tall, because look how close his head is to the top of that doorway!" When directors want you to see a character as smaller-than-life, they build a set with larger-than-normal doorways.

You'll find more truth in what you hear if you can determine the speaker's standard. What does it mean when a two-year-old says, "I met a really tall man?" What does it mean when a basketball player says the same thing?

If a friend asks, "Don't you just love a big city?", what does your friend mean by "big"? As big as New York? Or only slightly bigger than Truck Stop Junction?

TIP: Put *all* adjectives under your mental microscope. Does "deep" river mean deeper than a wading pool, but not as deep as the ocean? Is a "smart" dog smarter than Goofy, but not as smart as Lassie? Is an "interesting" museum less interesting than the Smithsonian, but more interesting than the trophy shelf in your uncle's den?

Comparisons help you discover the precise meaning of what you hear, read, or see. When someone tells you, "I am happy," that simply isn't enough information.

Comparisons can also create illusions and cause mistakes. When you see the moon on the horizon, it may look twice as large as it does in the sky. That's because you tend to compare its size to familiar objects. On the horizon, you compare it to trees and buildings, and it looks much larger. High in the sky, the moon appears small compared to the vastness of space.

- Look at the "big" horizon moon through a paper tube to block out surroundings. You'll find that it doesn't appear any larger than when it's above your head.

- Have you ever noticed the moon "following" you as you ride along in the family car? That's because you're comparing it to the objects whizzing past your point of vision. The moon isn't whizzing past, so it must be following you...or so it seems.

- Have you ever sat in a parked car when the car beside you began to roll slowly backwards? Did it seem like the car you were in was moving forward? That's because you mistakenly sized up the situation as "the *other* car is sitting still, so I must be rolling forward."

Your perception of time is also affected by comparisons. Sit and stare at a clock for three minutes; then do something you enjoy for the same amount of time. The second three minutes will pass much more quickly.

If you still aren't impressed by how comparisons shape your perceptions, try this experiment:

1. Find three containers for water.

2. Fill one with water that's as hot as you can stand to touch; one with very cold water; and one with lukewarm water.

3. Place the lukewarm water between the hot and cold.

4. Now plunge one hand into the hot water, and the other into the cold water. Leave your hands there for as long as you can bear it.

5. Then plunge both hands into the tepid water at the same time.

The hand that was in the cold water will feel the tepid water as "hot." The hand that was in the hot water will feel the tepid water as "cold." Both hands compare where they are to where they were.

You're constantly making comparisons in your search for the truth. Some comparisons, such as those which create sensory illusions (a big horizon moon), are subconscious and involuntary. Others are quite deliberate, such as when you decide to buy the "large" instead of the "jumbo" package of potato chips.

Whenever you make a decision or form an opinion, you are making some kind of comparison—good/bad, big/small, important/unimportant. Even "truth" is true only as compared to a lie.

WHAT DO YOU SEE?

1. Which curve is larger?

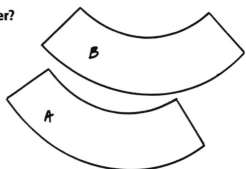

Both curves are the same size, but you see the one on the top as larger. This is because you judge the long outside of the top curve against the short inside of the bottom curve.

Experiment with this illusion. Copy the curves, cut them out, and place them side by side. Their sizes will seem to change with their positions.

2. Which lines are longer?

Is line 1 or 2 longer?

Lines 1 and 2 are the same length. The arrows on the ends influence what you see.

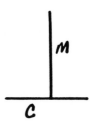

Is line C or M longer?

Lines C and M are the same length. Line M runs into Line C, giving Line C the look of 2 short lines. To make anything look taller and thinner, use vertical lines. To make anything look fatter and wider, use horizontal lines.

3. Are there gray spots at the intersections?

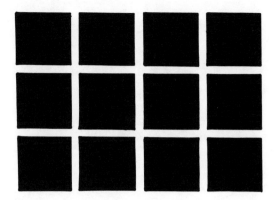

There seem to be spots at the intersections...but when you look right at them, they disappear.

The alleys between the blocks look ultra-white because they are closed in by so much black. When the four ultra-white alleys meet at an intersection, the area at the intersection appears to be gray because you are comparing it to the ultra-white.

The next time you buy a pair of white socks, put them beside an old, used pair of "white" socks and the old ones will look gray.

4. Which black circle is larger?

The circles are the same size. You see them as different sizes because you are comparing them with the "petals." Big petals make the center look small; small petals make the center look big.

5. Which stick is bigger?

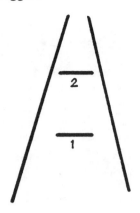

The sticks are the same size. You see them as different because the converging lines give the illusion of perspective and depth.

If two objects look the same size, but one appears to be farther away than the other, you will judge the "distant" object to be larger because you know that things always look smaller when they are farther away. Stick 2 seems to be farther away than Stick 1, so it appears to be larger.

HIDDEN MEANINGS

The truth is easier to recognize when a speaker, writer, or rule-maker tells you what standards he or she uses. For example, Mayor Bluto promises to make your town "prosperous." But what exactly is his standard of prosperous? Prosperous compared to what, and when?

Imagine that you receive a weekly allowance. You're worried that it might be cut off sometime soon. You voice your concern, and your parent says, "I won't let any child of mine do without an allowance she works hard to earn. You'll keep getting the allowance you deserve."

Whew! What a relief, you think...and then allowance day comes and goes and you don't get any. When you remind your parent, "You said you'd give me my allowance," your parent replies, "No, I said you'd get the allowance *you work to earn* and the allowance *you deserve*. You didn't do any work, so you don't deserve your allowance."

In July, 1981, many Americans were concerned that their monthly Social Security benefits might be reduced. In response, President Ronald Reagan said, "I will not stand by and see those of you who are dependent on Social Security deprived of the benefits you've worked so hard to earn. You will continue to receive your checks in the full amount due you."

What do you think he meant? Did the President support continuing the benefits, or reducing them?

According to David Gergen, Reagan's spokesperson at the time, the statement meant that the President would decide who was "dependent" on the benefits, who "earned" them, and who was "due" them. To get even closer to the truth, someone should have asked, "What are the President's standards for 'dependent,' 'earned,' and 'due'?"

The big fish in the little pond, and the little fish in the big pond, may be the same fish. So if a friendly fisherman tells you there are BIG fish in the Lake of Truth, you should find out his standard for "big" before you drive a hundred miles to go fishing. (Not that a fisherman would ever lie!)

PUTTING THINGS IN CONTEXT

Your perception also depends on the *context*, or surroundings, of information you receive. A newspaper means one thing in a library and another on the bottom of a bird cage.

Have you ever figured out the meaning of a word by looking at the rest of the sentence? Then you know how context can clear up confusion.

Have you ever found an item more appealing because you saw it in an exclusive store instead of a discount store? Then you know the power of context to change your mind.

Artists use out-of-context images to make bold statements. They may depict an indoor jungle, a lifeguard on a desert, a clown in a business suit, or a Cat in a Hat.

Cartoonists and comedians depend on out-of-context situations to get laughs. Gary Larson's *The Far Side* is funny because animals, insects, and people almost always appear out of context. The Marx Brothers were funny because they behaved outrageously in very formal settings.

While content *defines* truth, context *interprets* it. If truth depended only on content, then all instances of bread-stealing would be the same. Context leaves room for questions.

Was the bread stolen by somebody playing a prank? Was it stolen to feed starving children? Was it taken from the cupboard of a poor person who had no other food? Was it stolen just to be mean? Context gives the truth a little more flexibility.

"You don't invent the answers; you reveal the answers."

—Jonas Salk

CONTEXT INTERPRETS TRUTH

Read the word vertically and it's C-A-T. Read it horizontally and it's T-H-E. The middle symbol is an "H" or an "A" depending on the surrounding information, or context.

Read horizontally and you see A-B-C. Read vertically, and it's 12-13-14. The symbol in the center is either "B" or "13" depending on the context.

To recognize a lie, you must see things as they are, not as as they "should be" or as you want them to be. The illusion called the "proofreader's error" shows how natural it is for us to miss this fundamental truth.

You may have just committed that very error. Did you notice that the word "as" at the end of the first line in the last paragraph is repeated at the beginning of the second line? You probably read the text as if the extra "as" didn't exist. You saw what should be, not what is.

Most of the time, you can trust your senses to act in your best interests. For example, when you see something at an angle, such as an open door, the image on your retina is a distorted door. But to you it looks rectangular.

Fortunately, your mind adjusts sizes and shapes so they remain fairly constant. If it didn't, you'd live in a world of cattle which become tiny and doors which change shape. You'd run into things and generally be incapable of functioning well in the "real world."

Thanks to size and shape constancy, your senses bring you a more stable world. It isn't a true duplicate of the real world, but it is a sort of "lie" that works for you.

SIZE AND SHAPE CONSTANCY

If one door is shut, one partly open, and a third open even more, the image hitting your retina is different for each door. The wide-open door is not a rectangular image, yet you see it as a rectangle. Your brain automatically adjusts for distance and angle because you "know" what shape a door should be. This is called *shape constancy.*

Hold the circle about a foot away from you. Now extend your arm full length. Does the circle appear to be the same size in both cases?

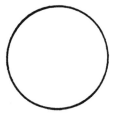

In fact, the image hitting your retina when the circle is 1 foot away is 4 times as large as when it is 2 feet away. But the circle probably looks the same size to you at both distances. This is called *size constancy.*

The brain has an amazing ability to adapt to a distorted world and its images.

AFTERIMAGES

Afterimages are another way illusions can give you a more accurate picture of the world. When you retain an image from one moment and combine it with the image of the next moment, your experience is a smooth flow rather than a lot of little pieces. If you saw the world as it really is, you wouldn't be able to function.

For example, movies don't move. A movie is a series of pictures shown at a very rapid rate. If it weren't for afterimages, movies wouldn't make sense.

Afterimages make it appear as if things are in motion when they really aren't. The brain decides if there is motion by asking:

- Do the eyes have to move to keep the object in view?
- Are there changes in the object's size, clarity, or color?
- How does the object compare to the background?

• •

**PHI PHENOMENON: When two lights flash about
.06 seconds apart and are seen as being in motion,
this is called *phi phenomenon*. This illusion is
what makes those big, fancy signs on stores,
restaurants, and casinos look so spectacular.**

• •

Your brain continually gathers tiny pieces of information,
examines them, and tries to give them meaning or fit them into
a larger pattern. Keep this in mind as you sniff out the truth.

AFTERIMAGE EXPERIMENTS

1. Stare at a red patch for about 45 seconds (try not to blink), then
look at a white wall or a white piece of paper. You will see a
green patch. Stare at a green patch, and you will see a red
afterimage. Yellow/Blue and Black/White will work the same way.

2. Cut a slit in an index card, or make vertical, horizontal, and
diagonal hatch marks on a piece of tracing paper. Lay the card
or tracing paper on a page of print. You should not be able to
read the words. Move the card or tracing paper back and forth
rapidly, and your brain puts the pieces together...you can read
the words. Move the card or tracing paper slowly and you can't
read the words.

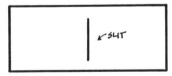

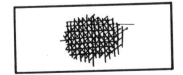

3. Rub two coins together rapidly between your thumb and forefinger. A third coin will appear.

4. Draw vertical lines on a plain index card. Poke a hole in the middle and spin it on the end of a pencil. The lines will look like circles.

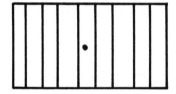

5. Try movie-making—a practical use for afterimages.

   a. Cut a piece of paper about 11″ long and 2″ wide.

   b. Fold it in half so it looks like a greeting card which opens from the bottom.

   c. Draw a simple picture on the inside, where the greeting would normally be. Close the card and trace the same picture on the front—*except change one thing.* For example, change a frowning face to a smiling one, or open eyes to closed eyes.

   d. Roll the top flap around a pencil (a little piece of tape to attach the pencil at the beginning of the roll helps).

   e. QUICKLY roll and unroll the top flap to see a moving picture.

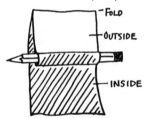

6. For a longer movie, draw a series of pictures, making a slight change in each picture. Flip through them with your thumb. You might use the outside margins of an unwanted book or magazine.

TRUSTING YOUR INSTINCTS

If a situation doesn't "feel" quite right to you, or you "sense" you aren't getting the whole truth, trust your instincts!

The same brain which fits pieces of information into a seamless pattern is also capable of picking up subtle clues which warn you of possible deception. Examples: body language, spoken language patterns, comments that don't "fit," behaviors which are slightly unexpected, and so on.

Maybe your dog, Snuffy, always barks at strangers, but the first time Mr. X comes to your door, Snuffy stays silent. Because this is a non-event, you may not consciously notice it. Later, though, you may find yourself thinking, "There's something about Mr. X that I just don't trust."

You may feel silly because you lack specific evidence against Mr. X. Trust your instincts! Vague feelings can be first-rate lie-detectors.

· ·

TROMP L'OEIL *(tromp l'oy)*: This French phrase literally means "fool the eye." It is used to describe effects in architecture, painting, and sculpture which are achieved by optical illusion.

· ·

CHANGING REALITY

Normally, common sense wouldn't let you get on an airplane. You have seen airplanes get smaller and smaller as they climb to the clouds. You have even watched them disappear.

But you have adjusted to these "lies" of your senses. Your brain makes sense of the distortions. You "know" the truth is that the plane only appears smaller because it is getting farther away.

You don't create reality, but you do change your reality by adjusting to the world as it is. This same wisdom will serve you well as you encounter other lies.

Now that you know that 100% absolute, all-the-time, total truth is impossible, you can enjoy your life (and the following chapters) using your senses and your common sense.

CHAPTER 3

BE TRUE TO YOURSELF

- -

**Hold this page about 14" in front of you. Close
your left eye and look directly at the rabbit with
your right eye. What don't you see?**

ANSWER: **The spot where the bear is will appear blank because of
the blind spot in your field of vision. Any object in your blind spot is
invisible to you.**

- -

SELF-LIES AND BLIND SPOTS

You're invited to a friend's party. You don't want to go. So you tell yourself, "I have a headache tonight. I think I'll stay home."

You really should clean out your closet. It's been weeks...months...years. You open the door, look inside, and say, "I'll do it tomorrow." But you know you won't.

You may be surprised to discover that you have a blind spot in your field of vision. You may be surprised to learn that you lie to yourself. Like the bear in your blind spot, self-lies are truths you can't see.

If you're like most people (and most people are), you tell yourself that you're a logical person. Then you go on to behave in emotional and illogical ways.

Did you just accept the suggestion that "most people" act a certain way? If so, you didn't use your logic. A logical person would ask, "What exactly do you mean by *most people,* and how do you *know* what they tell themselves?" "I am logical" is another self-lie.

"Just one cookie"..."I can quit any time"..."This one doesn't count"..."One more time"..."It can't happen to me"...all are self-lies.

When you lie to yourself, you're the liar and the lied to. You divide your thinking into two "yous." One becomes the rabbit, and the other becomes the bear, invisible in the way you see yourself.

SOME REASONS WHY YOU LIE TO YOURSELF

Why would you lie to yourself, the one person in the world you should be totally truthful with? Because lying to yourself can be an escape.

There may be realities in your life you think you can't deal with, or you aren't yet ready to deal with. You may want to avoid taking responsibility for something you have done or haven't done, something you want to do or don't want to do. Lying offers a way out—maybe not forever, but for now.

Or maybe you want to be "the best." It's easy to progress from 1) wanting to be *your* best to 2) wanting to be better than other people to 3) wanting to be better than reality allows. When this happens, you must lie to yourself constantly. You can't be yourself anymore.

In "The Secret Life of Walter Mitty," a short story by James Thurber, a humble little man weaves elaborate fantasies of passion and adventure. Pinocchio dreams of being a "real boy." The Little Mermaid dreams of being a "real girl." The Velveteen Rabbit dreams of becoming "real." At times, we all want to be someone or something we aren't. There's nothing wrong with dreaming, as long as we don't lose touch with who and what we really are.

Some self-lies can be dangerous. When girls believe they can look like Barbie dolls, and boys believe they can become super-hero hunks, they may starve themselves or abuse their bodies to the point of illness or death. Other people may turn to diet pills, hair dyes, tanning salons, cosmetic surgery, and more in an effort to live their self-lies.

FOUR WAYS YOU LIE TO YOURSELF

How can you manage to lie to yourself, the one person in the world you can't hide from? There are at least four ways.

1. By *creating impossible situations for yourself.*

You learned about the research paper on the first day of the semester. Every day since then, you put off getting started. Now it's the night before the paper is due. You read the requirements and admit to yourself, "I can't possibly get this done."

It's your decision to do or not to do your school work. But it's a lie to claim that you have "too much work." It's dishonest to complain about consequences you knew would come. Or maybe you kept them hidden in your blind spot.

2. By *ignoring the facts.*

You know that your favorite snack food is loaded with chemicals and preservatives that could be harmful to your health. But you decide not to worry about it. After all, you have to eat!

3. By *denying the facts.*

You read that the government allows only so many rodent hairs in packaged food products. From this, you could reason that there are at least *some* rodent hairs in your favorite snack food. But you decide that it must be the exception.

"I am now nearly 18, and I realize that my desire to be skinny was heavily influenced by Barbie. The pervasiveness of this image has probably contributed to the high incidence of eating disorders in our society. Anorexia and bulimia are dangerous, frightening and potentially fatal diseases. I should know; it happened to me."

—A teenage girl in a letter to a newspaper editor

4. By making promises you know you can't or won't keep.

You accept an invitation to a party, knowing you won't go. You offer to help a relative move, knowing you won't be around or you'll be too busy.

This kind of self-lie has one of two causes. First, you want to appear agreeable to other people. You want people to like you and to see you as a sociable, helpful person.

Or second, you're too afraid to say "no" on the spot. You put it off until later, when you can invent a really good excuse.

> TRUTH #2:
> YOU'LL SAVE YOURSELF A LOT OF TROUBLE
> BY FOLLOWING THESE TWO
> SIMPLE GUIDELINES:
> 1. DON'T SAY "NO" WHEN YOU MEAN "YES."
> 2. DON'T SAY "YES" WHEN YOU MEAN "NO."

Like cheating at solitaire, lying to yourself usually doesn't hurt anyone but you. So go ahead and lie a little. Just be sure to balance your self-lies with plenty of self-truths. And be aware of the probable consequences of your self-lies.

LITTLE WHITE LIES YOU TELL YOURSELF

Some self-lies are harmless. For instance, you're out shopping when you notice a new jacket. You tell yourself, "I *need* that jacket." Depending on your financial circumstances, this is a harmless self-lie.

You could ask yourself whether you really "need" the jacket. If you don't already own one, then you probably do need it to keep warm. But if you already have four jackets and you're still insisting that you "need" the new one, then you really don't—or else you "need" it for some other reason. Maybe you think it will help you to feel accepted by your peer group.

"I don't know how it happens, my car just drives itself to Neiman Marcus."

—Victoria Principal

Why ask why you're lying to yourself? Because you may come up with a better way to win acceptance. You may realize that you don't want to be accepted based on what you wear. And, as a bonus, you'll save money!

> **TRUTH #3:**
> **MOST OF THE THINGS YOU BUY AREN'T NEARLY AS ATTRACTIVE THREE MONTHS LATER, OUT OF THE PACKAGE AND OUT OF THE STORE. KEEP THIS IN MIND AND YOU'LL PASS UP A LOT OF FOOLISH PURCHASES.**

Another harmless self-lie is the belief that you can watch a sporting event at home and cheer your team on to victory. You think that you can influence the outcome just by sitting in front of the TV. Of course you can't, but it's fun to pretend.

You also know that it's not logical to get excited because highly-paid athletes are winning a game for your "home team." They would play for whichever team paid them the most money.

When you go to a movie, you're aware that you're being lied to. You agree in advance to accept illusions—monsters, superheroes, people jumping out of windows and blowing up trains. This is a harmless self-lie, an escape into entertainment.

TRUE OR FALSE?

1. Diamonds are rare gems of great value.

2. Giving a diamond engagement ring is an old English custom.

Find the answers on page **153**.

We tell ourselves that certain things have value beyond their real worth. Would you pay $5,250 for Madonna's old sneakers, the price they sold for at an auction? What makes your great-grandfather's farm more valuable to you than the farm across the road? What if you suddenly discovered that the house you live in was built on the spot where Abraham Lincoln camped when he was a boy?

Even our money has value only because we all agree that it does. A $20 bill is really just a piece of paper. If another government took over, it could declare that $20 bill worthless.

Value is whatever you tell yourself it is. You could go to a second-hand store tomorrow, find an interesting piece of junk for $3, and tell yourself that your favorite famous person once owned it. Suddenly that piece of junk would be "valuable" to you.

IN OTHER'S WORDS

Millie's Book: As Dictated to Barbara Bush was published in 1990. Its author was listed as "Mildred K. Bush." Mildred K. Bush is a dog.

Everybody knew that Millie hadn't really written the book. Yet millions of people went along with the illusion. It was fun to imagine a dog's-eye view of life in the White House.

In 1989, a group called Milli Vanilli won the Grammy Award for Best New Artist. Soon it was discovered that the members of the group hadn't really sung their own songs. They had only lip-synched them. The discovery caused a scandal. Millions of people felt cheated and deceived.

Which deceptions are okay, and which are not okay? The standard for truth is not always clear. We accept Millie, but reject Milli Vanilli. The difference seems to lie in whether we know about the deception in advance. Then we can choose to go along or go the other way.

But we aren't always aware when people use words that aren't their own. Many famous people have their "autobiographies" written by ghostwriters. Most politicians have speech writers prepare speeches for them.

During his 1988 presidential campaign, George Bush pledged "no net loss of wetlands." After he was elected, he appeared to break that promise. Richard Darman, director of the Office of Management and Budget, explained, "[President Bush] didn't say that. He read what was given to him in a speech."

For years, environmentalists have rallied behind a famous speech supposedly made by Chief Seattle in 1854. The speech is very beautiful and inspiring. Here is part of what it says:

> Every part of this earth is sacred to my people....If all the beasts were gone, men would die from a great loneliness of spirit. For whatever happens to the beasts soon happens to the man....The earth does not belong to man; man belongs to the earth....All things are connected like the blood which unites one family....Whatever befalls the earth befalls the sons of the earth. Man does not weave the web of life; he is merely a strand in it....

In fact, this speech was written by a man named Ted Perry in the early 1970's for a film script. Perry explains that he tried to imagine what Chief Seattle *might have said*. When Perry's name was left off the film credits, the speech became known as "Chief Seattle's Speech."

Can you think of other examples of lip-synching and ghostwriting? Which ones are you willing to accept and lie to yourself about? Which ones leave you feeling cheated and deceived? In your opinion, should politicians write their own speeches? Why or why not?

TIME TRAVELS

Many people get anxious as they approach their thirtieth or fortieth birthday. Why don't they get more anxious about their thirty-third or forty-second birthday? Because some birthdays seem to have greater significance than others.

Turning ten may have had special meaning for you—your first double-digit birthday. When you turned thirteen, you may have felt that you were no longer a child.

But you don't really age a whole year on any birthday. You don't "grow up" from one birthday to the next. You are exactly one day older than you were the day before, and one minute older than the previous minute.

Have you ever made New Year's resolutions? Many people see January 1 as a chance to start their lives over. They promise to break old, bad habits on that day. They think this gives them permission to eat too much, drink too much, and exercise too little during the holidays leading up to New Year's Day. Even if they make the same promise every year, they still believe that "this year will be different."

In fact, every year contains many "years." There's the New Year, which begins on different days for different people. There's the fiscal year, which companies and governments use to plan their budgets; it usually begins in July. There's the school year, which begins in September.

CHOOSE YOUR NEW YEAR

happp Acm Brar

New Year's festivals have been celebrated around the world for more than 5,000 years. But when exactly is New Year's Day? That depends on your century, culture, and religion.

- The ancient Egyptians began the year with the autumnal equinox—around September 23 on our calendar.

- The Romans celebrated their New Year on March 1 until 153 B.C.

- In early Medieval times, most European Christians called March 25 New Year's Day—except for Anglo-Saxon Christians, who preferred December 25.

- The Jewish New Year begins on Rosh Hashana, the first day of the month of Tishri—sometime in September or early October.

- The Chinese New Year falls between January 10 and February 19.

- The Muslim New Year comes on the first day of the month of Muharram, which varies from year to year, since Muslim months are lunar.

- March 21 is New Year's Day in Iran.

You could declare your own New Year's Day, and it wouldn't really matter when it fell. The way we measure time is another self-deception.

For more than 1500 years, many people measured time by the Julian calendar. In 1582, Pope Gregory XIII changed the Julian calendar by subtracting 10 days from it. This made up for a mathematical miscalculation regarding Leap Year.

People fought the change because they believed that subtracting days from the calendar year would shorten their lives. Russia refused to accept the new Gregorian calendar—named after Pope Gregory—until 1918. When the American colonies adopted it in 1752, George Washington's birthday moved from February 11 to February 22 because of eleven days lost in February.

April Fool's Day, the day officially set aside for lying, exists because of a calendar change. In 1564, the reformed calendar of Charles IX, King of France, shifted the New Year celebration from April 1 to January 1. People who kept celebrating the New Year on April 1 were called "April Fools."

In our time, calendars are lengthened and shortened (Leap Year), and clocks are moved ahead and back (Daylight Savings Time), but we still celebrate events that happened "ten years ago today." When we can account for time, we feel as if we have some control over it. We're fooling ourselves, but there's no real harm done.

Even the way we experience time is a self-deception. In countries such as Mexico, people take a siesta at noon. This is a sensible way to spend the hottest part of the day. In some European countries, people are expected to take long lunches. But in the United States, midday rests and lengthy lunches are perceived as "wasting time." People in the U.S. view time as a tangible object which must not be "wasted."

FOOD FALSEHOODS

When you see a report about the additives and pesticides present in food today, do you read it or ignore it? When you see a TV program about factory farming, do you watch it or change the channel?

Gourmets go to elegant restaurants and dine on escargot, caviar, sushi, and steak tartare. They probably don't tell themselves that they're really munching snails, fish eggs, raw fish, and raw ground-up beef with raw egg on top.

TRUE OR FALSE?

1. Carrots improve your eyesight.

2. Spinach makes you strong.

3. Chocolate causes acne.

Find the answers on pages **153-154**.

If you didn't lie to yourself about what you eat and drink, you'd soon lose a lot of weight. Where does your water come from? Shiny faucets or bottles. Few people in industrialized countries still carry their water in buckets from the nearest (polluted) lake or stream. Where does your food come from? Unless you live on a farm, you probably buy all or most of it at a grocery store.

Food companies make their products attractive and de-emphasize the negatives. They wrap raw meat in clear plastic, put cheese in colorful cartons or boxes, and package eggs in cardboard or styrofoam holders.

Often, the food in advertisements isn't even real food. Because real food doesn't photograph well under hot lights, advertising agencies use white glue for the milk on cereal, shaving cream for whipped cream, and a squirt of detergent in cocoa to make it foamy.

LOGIC OR EXCUSES?

Self-lies often come from the human drive to make our beliefs match our behaviors. Experiments in social psychology show that when you behave in a way that conflicts with your beliefs, you experience an inner tension called *cognitive dissonance*.

For instance, if you don't believe in lying, and you suddenly hear yourself lying to someone, you'll feel uncomfortable because you're violating your own belief. This feeling is so intense that you will eventually change either your behavior or your belief to make the two "match." Guess which one people usually change?

In one experiment, students were asked about their beliefs on cheating. Later, they were given an opportunity to cheat on a test. The ones who cheated decided that cheating wasn't so bad after all. The ones who resisted the temptation to cheat decided that cheating was even worse than they had originally believed.

We behave emotionally, then invent logical "reasons" for our behavior. Emotion, like *Star Trek*'s Captain Kirk, keeps the action moving ahead, while logic, like Mr. Spock, follows one step behind, trying to make sense of it all.

Logic applied after the fact can turn almost anything into "the right thing to do." And when we get really good at making up logical reasons for our actions, we stop worrying about whether they're right or wrong.

WOULD YOU BELIEVE....

Insurance companies hear the most amazing excuses. Here are just a few reported by the Omaha Property and Casualty Insurance Company and State Farm Insurance Companies in Bloomington, Illinois:

- "Coming home, I drove into the wrong house and collided with a tree I don't have."

- "The guy was all over the road. I had to swerve a number of times before I hit him."

- "I pulled away from the side of the road, glanced at my mother-in-law, and headed over the embankment."

- "An invisible car came out of nowhere, struck my vehicle, and vanished."

- "I drove my truck under a bridge, and it didn't fit."

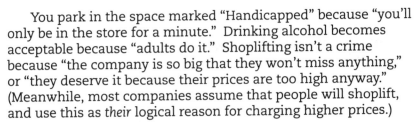

You park in the space marked "Handicapped" because "you'll only be in the store for a minute." Drinking alcohol becomes acceptable because "adults do it." Shoplifting isn't a crime because "the company is so big that they won't miss anything," or "they deserve it because their prices are too high anyway." (Meanwhile, most companies assume that people will shoplift, and use this as *their* logical reason for charging higher prices.)

When is a logical reason reasonable, and when is it simply convenient? You decide. To check for truth, ask, "Am I excusing myself for doing something I want to do?" Or, "Am I giving myself permission to do something I want to do?" Or use real logic and ask yourself, "What would the world be like if everyone did what I just did, or what I'm about to do?"

Excuses can help you feel better about yourself. "I would have done the dishes, but I had so much homework"..."I would have sent a birthday present, but I knew you'd rather get a phone call"....Excuses give the appearance that you're "doing your best" when you're just being lazy. They let you off the hook—at least, in your own mind.

What's wrong with that? Eventually, people will stop depending on you. Who wants to be around someone who is always making excuses?

GOOD EXCUSES

Not all excuses are bad. Some can actually be good for you!

- In the 1980's, researchers at the University of Kansas found that people who make excuses are healthier and have higher self-esteem than people who blame themselves when things go wrong. They perform better on mental and physical tests. They tend to view bad times as temporary, giving them a more hopeful outlook on life.

- In another study, researchers found that baseball players who took credit for good performances lived longer than those who didn't. So did players who attributed poor performances to "outside causes." In other words, "I got that home run because I'm a great hitter...but I struck out because the pitcher was lousy."

- Students improved their reading and math performance when their teachers encouraged them to make the excuse, "I wasn't trying hard enough."

- Some excuses give you greater self-confidence and more control over your life by pointing out ways you might improve. "I failed the test because I didn't study" is an excuse with a use: next time, study!

WHO'S TO BLAME?

We use blame for the same reason we use excuses: because it works. Even a two-year-old knows that you can protect yourself from unpleasant consequences if you can find someone or something to blame, or at least someone who is *more* guilty, or who "did it first."

Have you ever said "It was his fault" or "She started it"? If you haven't, you may not be human!

Blame can get you out of a sticky situation. But while it removes responsibility, it also removes personal power. If you say, "Look what he made me do," you are claiming that another person controlled your actions. You are playing the role of a helpless victim, unable to influence the course of your own life.

Not all blame is directed toward others. Some people blame themselves for everything. If they plan an outdoor event and it rains, *they* feel responsible. This self-lie puts pressure on them to create perfection in a world where perfection isn't possible.

Many common words and phrases express this theme of self-blame for things beyond our control. For example, we say, "I caught a cold," not "a cold caught me."

In most cases, blame is a waste of time. If someone bumps your arm and you knock over a glass of milk, you can spend an hour blaming and trying to convince the other person to clean it up. Or you can take five minutes to clean it up yourself. Maybe the other person will help, and you can do it in two minutes.

When things go wrong in your life, you can blame your school, your teachers, your parents, your coach, your friends, the government...the list goes on and on. Or you can recognize that you have the power to make life better for yourself. Remember the Nike slogan: JUST DO IT!

Blame postpones or prevents positive decisions and actions. When you're busy looking for someone to blame for a problem, you have the illusion that you're doing something about it. But even if you find someone to blame, that won't solve anything unless the "guilty" person agrees that 1) the problem really is his or her fault, and 2) he or she will do something about it.

If there's a problem in your life that needs fixing, which is the better solution: to find out who "caused" it and try to "make" that person fix it, or to find out who else wants it fixed and work together for a common goal?

- Find a newspaper article in which two people or groups are blaming each other for a problem. Try to think of a better way to handle the situation. Write a letter to the editor proposing your solution.

- For two or three days in a row, read the letters to the editor in your daily newspaper. Look for the ones that have to do with problems. Which do you find more of: blaming letters, or solution-proposing letters?

- If blame didn't exist, how might the world be different today? How might history be different? How would political campaigns be run? Would a blameless world be better or worse?

THE NO-FAULT FAMILY AGREEMENT

Copy this agreement on a sheet of paper. Invite your family to read and sign it with you. At the end of the week, check to see how it affected your family. Did you get more accomplished? Did you have fewer arguments? Did you feel better about yourselves individually, and as a family?

WE, THE (NAME)_____ *FAMILY,*

AGREE THAT FOR THE WEEK OF (MONTH)_____

(DAY)_____, (YEAR)_____ *THROUGH*

(MONTH)_____ (DAY)_____, (YEAR)_____,

NO FAMILY MEMBER WILL BLAME ANY OTHER FAMILY MEMBER FOR ANYTHING.

SIGNED:

_____

_____

_____

_____

NO EXCEPTIONS

You've seen them on the evening news. They stare into the camera and say, "You never think things like this will happen to you," or, "You think things like this can only happen to *other people.*"

Perhaps like you, they have told themselves, "I'm the exception to the rule." This self-lie convinces us that *other people* win lotteries and sweepstakes, have houses burn to the ground, live to be 125, or die young, but not us! Yet we buy lottery tickets, enter sweepstakes, purchase fire insurance, and write last wills and testaments. Maybe, deep down inside, we realize that we're not the exception.

One of the most dangerous self-lies goes like this: "Because I am not like other people, I am not subject to the laws of society, or even to the laws of nature." Intellectually, we know better, but emotionally we believe that we're somehow "outside" the things that apply to all those "other people."

This belief can lead to irresponsible and even harmful behaviors. For example, you may waste water, throw litter onto the street, or drive too fast. Since you're not "other people," you may feel that your individual actions don't make any difference, and they don't have the same consequences as when "other people" do them.

In 1991, Lakers basketball star Magic Johnson announced that he had tested positive for the HIV virus. People everywhere were stunned, and many were heard to say, "If it can happen to him, it can happen to anybody—even me." For the first time, they counted themselves among the "other people" at risk for AIDS.

TAKING SIDES

Sometimes the belief that "I am not like other people" evolves into the self-lie that "I am better than other people."

It's one thing to tell yourself that you can *perform* better than someone else; if you can run faster or write better stories, great—take the credit due you. But it's quite another thing to tell yourself that you *are* better than an entire group of people because of your race, sex, nationality, religion, social class, or name.

If your claim is specific, measurable, and performance-based—"I can jump higher than anyone else in my P.E. class"—then it isn't a self-lie. You're comparing your performance against that of certain individuals, not a whole group of people who may never get the chance to compete against you.

If your claim is general, untestable, and based on so-called "natural" superiority—"I can jump higher than any girl my age"—then it's a very big and dangerous self-lie.

"I am better than other people" is a lie born in self-doubt. Only when people feel insecure about themselves do they feel the need to prove that they are superior to others.

When Mother Teresa works with the poor and the sick, she's too busy doing important things to worry about how superior she may or may not be. Saying that "men are better than women" or "women are better than men" doesn't obligate you to do anything to prove yourself. The implication is that you were "born" superior.

"I am firm. You are obstinate. He is a pigheaded fool."

–Katherine Whitehorn

A SELF-LIE TEST

Take this test yourself. Then give it to at least four other people before you attempt to score it.

True or false?

1. I am more sensitive than most people.

2. I am more thoughtful than most people.

3. I work harder than most people.

4. I have more troubles than most people.

5. I am luckier than most people.

6. I am more capable than most people.

7. I try harder than most people.

8. I am busier than most people.

9. I am more caring than most people.

10. I am more honest than most people.

For tips on scoring, see page **154**.

During the 1930's and 1940's, a group of people convinced themselves that they, the members of the Aryan "race," were a superior, "master" race, and they set out to give their claims the appearance of "scientific validity." If they could not prove their claims scientifically, they would just impose their will on the world. As a direct result of this massive self-lie, millions of people died in World War II.

In fact, there is no such thing as an Aryan "race." There is only an Aryan language. The Aryan "race" was a lie from the start.

When one race claims superiority, it always follows that other races are labeled "inferior." The self-proclaimed "superior" race feels justified in persecuting, enslaving, or even eliminating the "inferior" races.

How can you tell when people are convinced of their own superiority? Listen to the way they use the words "we" and "they," and how often. Ask them to define "we" and "they." In this way, you may expose their true feelings. People who feel superior are people you should avoid.

"WE"-"THEY" PING-PONG

Invite some friends to play this game with you. Divide into a "WE" team and a "THEY" team. The "WE" team serves first ("WE are easy-going"). The "THEY" team has 5 seconds to respond with a THEY phrase meaning essentially the same thing, but with a negative sound and meaning ("THEY are lazy").

See how long you can keep up the game. Make up your own specific rules. Here are some examples to get you started.

WE are easy-going.	THEY are lazy.
WE are entrepreneurial.	THEY are greedy.
WE are sophisticated.	THEY are snobbish.
WE are thrifty.	THEY are cheap.
WE are intelligent.	THEY are eggheads.
WE are well-dressed.	THEY are superficial.
WE are generous.	THEY are wasteful.
WE are boisterous.	THEY are noisy.
WE are cautious.	THEY are fearful.
WE are brave.	THEY are foolhardy.

Do you see the world in terms of "we" and "they"? How do you define these words? Are you thinking clearly? Are you being honest with yourself? Are you trying to hide your weaknesses within a larger identity, such as a race? Are you going along with a group instead of standing up for your own beliefs?

The things people hate most about "they" are often the same things they secretly fear about themselves. A person who feels weak may despise weakness in others.

APPEARANCES CAN BE DECEIVING

It would seem impossible to lie to yourself about being thin or good-looking or smart. Shouldn't you be able to look in the mirror or review your accomplishments for a quick reality check? As it turns out, not always.

Very thin people sometimes believe they are very fat. This condition, called *anorexia nervosa*, can become serious and even life-threatening. Some people with eating disorders literally starve themselves to death. They force themselves to throw up after they eat. Nothing can convince them that they are thin—not a mirror or a scale or a friend.

Good-looking people may convince themselves that they are ugly. Pop star Michael Jackson has radically changed his appearance by having plastic surgery several times. Elizabeth Taylor, Cher, Melanie Griffith, Kenny Rogers, Melissa Gilbert, La Toya Jackson, and Sylvester Stallone have all had plastic surgery.

Highly gifted people may feel like failures or frauds. Two out of five high achievers experience the "impostor phenomenon"—a deep-seated belief that they are fakes. They credit their success to good luck, charm, or chance rather than their own hard work and talent. They live in fear that someone will expose them as "ordinary"—just like all of those "other people."

What you tell yourself about yourself can hurt you or help you. It depends on what you say. Self-deception can turn potential success into failure, but it can also turn potential failure into success.

IN SEARCH OF THE LOST TRUTH

It's hard to tickle yourself and laugh. It's almost as hard to lie to yourself and believe yourself. But once you start accepting your self-lies and living with them every day, they become your reality. Eventually they are nearly impossible to change, or even to see. You have developed a blind spot.

At some point in your life, you may want to find a truth you've lost along the way. Logic won't be much help. Instead, listen for that "little voice" inside you that remembers the truth. It will be there when you need it—when you're tired of excuses, reasons, and blame. If you discover that helpful, harmful, and fun self-lies have somehow gotten all tangled up together, you can call on your feelings to sort them out.

Your feelings may tell you the truth when you *need* to hear it, even if you don't *want* to hear it. Messages from your inner voice saying, "This doesn't feel quite right," "That feels unsafe," or "I'm not my best self in this situation or around that person," are all worth listening to. So are physical messages including butterflies in your stomach, tension headaches, nervous sweats, shivers, or a dry mouth.

Pay attention to these signals from your feelings. Usually they contain some truth you need to hear.

"What one is, is of far greater importance than what one appears to be."

—Emily Post

"If you think you can, you can. And if you think you can't, you're right."

—Mary Kay Ash

"The germs of all truth lie in the soul, and when the ripe moment comes, the truth within answers to the fact without as the flower responds to the sun, giving it form for heat and color for light."

—Hamilton W. Mabie

BEING HUMAN

So you have excuses, blaming, fun self-lies, harmful self-lies, and helpful self-lies all mixed up somewhere inside of you. How did this happen?

When you were one year old, you didn't lie to yourself or worry about being late, looking foolish, or acting selfish. You just did what you did and that was that. Your actions didn't need reasons. Your mistakes didn't need explanations.

At some point, you discovered that reasons and excuses could get you out of trouble or get you what you wanted. By the time you were twelve, you were making excuses for the same things you did when you were five *without* excuses.

Adults started expecting and demanding that you behave logically. They asked you questions—"Why are you doing that?" "What does your drawing mean?" "Why did you color the dog purple?"—and you started questioning yourself. It became a habit to defend your actions with excuses, blaming, exceptions, and distortions.

Self-lies arise out of an inner battle between logic and emotions, "should" and "want to," perfect and imperfect, ideal and real, the need to be right and the need to be honest. Weighing your position on self-lies will always be a balancing act between logic and feelings. This balancing act is the key to eliminating your blind spots.

1. For each self-lie you catch yourself telling, ask yourself, "Is it harmless, harmful, or helpful to me and others?"

2. Try to determine why you told the self-lie. To avoid taking a risk? To appear perfect? To protect yourself or your self-image? Ask yourself, "Do I really 'need' the protection this self-lie provides?" Sometimes the answer will be "yes."

3. Weigh your desire for logic. Are you using too much or too little?

4. Take your emotional temperature. Are you letting your emotions rule? Or are you ignoring them and not giving them a proper hearing?

5. Try to predict the probable consequences of your self-lies, especially the ones you use all the time. Are they likely to have no effect, change you for the better, change you for the worse, change others for the better, change others for the worse, change your emotions, change your behavior, prod you into action?

Keep in mind that logic *and* emotions both have a place in the truth. Logic makes you appear rational and protects your self-image, but feelings keep you human. In the end, only you know what's true for you. Be true to your knowing self.

"If there were no falsehood in the world, there would be no doubt; if there were no doubt, there would be no inquiry; if no inquiry, no wisdom, no knowledge, no genius."

—Walter Savage Landor

CHAPTER 4

SOCIAL LIES

CARD A   **CARD B**

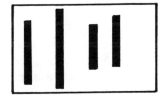   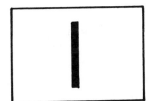

Which line on card A is the same length as the line on card B?

EXPERIMENT: **Cover up these words and show this to a friend. Then see if you can get your friend to change his or her original answer. Ask your friend the question again in a group of people who have agreed ahead of time to give a wrong answer.**

GETTING APPROVAL, GETTING AHEAD

Trees don't care what other trees think of them. Dogs, cats, and blades of grass aren't concerned about peer approval. But people need to be accepted by other people.

We seem to have a built-in desire to *be liked* by others, and also to *be like* others—to conform. This explains the Card A-Card B experiment, and many others as well.

- In 1934, people were shown a pinpoint of light in a dark room and asked to judge how much the light had "moved." (The light hadn't really "moved" at all. Because the eye is in constant motion, the light only *appeared* to move. This eye movement is what makes stars "twinkle.")

When they were told what others in the experiment had guessed, many people changed their original guess to match what the unknown "others" had said. They distorted their own perceptions to conform to majority opinion.

If self-lies are a balance of logic and emotion, the lies we tell others are a balance of the need for approval and the need to get ahead. It isn't easy to make people like us at the same time we're competing with them. But we try.

Imagine that you've just lost a volleyball game. You smile and tell the other team, "The sun was in my eyes." What are you really saying? First, that your *real* abilities are greater when the sun isn't in your eyes—a bid for approval. And second, that you could have won if only the sun hadn't been in your eyes—a competitive challenge. The game is over, but you're still playing it.

In a famous story called "The Emperor's New Clothes," dishonest men sell a gullible Emperor some cloth they claim is "magnificent to behold" but "invisible to fools." In fact, there is no cloth. Fearful of seeming foolish, the Emperor pretends to see it anyway.

If the story ended there, the Emperor's pretense would be just another polite social lie.

LIES OF CONVENIENCE

Dozens of times each day, we tell convenient but meaningless social lies. These may be compliments ("I love your new haircut!") or excuses ("Sorry I'm late; I had a flat tire").

Each kind serves a purpose. Saying nothing about an obvious change (a haircut) might imply, "I don't like it." Being late without making an excuse might suggest, "I don't think you're important."

This informal social code makes real compliments less meaningful ("Does he like my haircut, or is he just saying that?"). It makes real excuses less believable ("I've heard that flat-tire story before").

The lie of convenience is a shorthand way of appearing friendly and interested without getting involved in a real conversation. It's a kind of social code. "How are you?" means "Hi," and "I'm fine, how are you?" means "Hi back." Most people don't respond to "How are you?" with a serious answer, because the social code calls for the programmed answer, "I'm fine. How are you?"

You might use lies of convenience to keep the peace, or to create a certain image for yourself. You might pretend to agree with someone just to avoid an argument.

The Emperor might have used a lie of convenience to get rid of the shifty peddlers and their nonexistent cloth. But, as the story goes, he didn't.

How much polite or convenient lying is acceptable or desirable? You decide. A certain amount seems necessary to get along in the world.

You pretend not to notice the zit on a friend's nose, or you claim to like a classmate's new shoes when you secretly think they look stupid. These seem like caring behaviors, and you ask yourself, "What harm can they do?" You don't perceive these as serious "lies" but rather as "soft truths" or "little white lies."

"I never know how much of what I say is true."

—Bette Midler

PROTECTIVE LIES

Suppose that instead of pretending to like a person's *shoes*, you pretend to like the *person* because he or she can be useful to you.

You're not just being polite anymore. You're expecting something in return.

Take the Emperor, for instance. He doesn't go along with the phony salesmen to be polite. He doesn't admire the invisible cloth to spare their feelings. He buys it and has it sewn into a new suit, which he "wears" in a parade through the village! He expects the suit to enhance his image as Emperor.

The whole time the suit is being sewn, nobody speaks the truth because nobody wants to seem foolish. They *act* like fools so they won't *look* like fools. Appearance and acceptance have become more important than the truth.

By now, the lie has gone beyond convenience. It has become a lie of protection.

We tell protective lies when we feel threatened. We use them to defend ourselves and people we care about against the truth, and to satisfy our own need for approval.

When your little brother kicks your new neighbor, you say, "He isn't usually like that." When your friend embarrasses you in front of a group, you explain, "She gets a little irritable when she's tired." When the Emperor parades past, you say, "His Highness hasn't been himself lately."

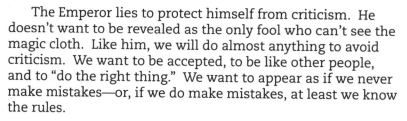

The Emperor lies to protect himself from criticism. He doesn't want to be revealed as the only fool who can't see the magic cloth. Like him, we will do almost anything to avoid criticism. We want to be accepted, to be like other people, and to "do the right thing." We want to appear as if we never make mistakes—or, if we do make mistakes, at least we know the rules.

So we *say*, "I was late because my alarm clock didn't go off," or "I didn't write a thank-you note because I was too busy with finals," or "I didn't use my salad fork because it was dirty." But we *mean*, "I know I should be on time" or "write thank-you notes" or "use my salad fork." Even if we don't do what we should, we let people know that we can.

COVER-UP LIES

Cover-up lies are small admissions of weakness that hide bigger weaknesses. They also free us from tasks we don't want to tackle.

We *say*, "I'm not good at math," but we *mean*, "I think I'm failing math," or "I hate studying for math quizzes." We *say*, "I have no sense of direction," but we *mean*, "I'm totally lost," or "I don't want to stop and read the map." We *say*, "I have no mechanical ability," but we *mean*, "I know nothing about cars," or "I don't want to be responsible for taking care of the car."

In a sneakier version of the cover-up lie, we *say*, "You're so good at washing windows" or "doing dishes" or "writing poems," but we *mean*, "Will you do it for me?"

The Emperor's advisors might have *said*, "I don't know anything about fashion, Sire." Or, "I'm no good at picking out clothes for you." But they would have *meant*, "Don't expect *us* to tell you the truth! We're not going to risk making you look foolish."

JUST KIDDING!

"Just kidding" is another common cover-up lie. When we say or do something that gets a negative reaction, we immediately laugh and insist, "Of course, I was just kidding!" Supposedly this cancels what we just said or did.

Compare this to a government "news leak," in which an "unidentified source" makes a claim or releases information. If the public reacts positively, the leak is held up as the truth; if the public reacts negatively, the leak is denied (just kidding!).

When the Emperor finally realized that he was walking around with no clothes on, the crooked salesmen might have smiled at him and said, "Just kidding!"

This lie implies that a particular event happened in a sort of "parallel reality." How can you get angry when a friend insults you if he was just kidding? How can you get upset at a classmate who steals your favorite pencil, then hands it back and claims she was just kidding? True, this can be confusing and frustrating. But hey—lighten up! Can't you take a joke?

HONESTY AND POWER

As the Emperor rides through the town stark naked, the people cheer and praise his "beautiful new clothes."

Have you ever told a friend that a new outfit looked great when you really thought it looked silly? Imagine that you're shopping together, and your friend tries on the outfit and asks for your opinion. What will you say?

Now imagine that your friend has already bought the outfit and is wearing it at a party. That pretty much describes the Emperor's situation. He has already bought his "new clothes;" now he's "wearing" them in a parade. What can his subjects say or do? It's already too late.

But one child doesn't know enough not to speak the truth. He shouts, "Look, the Emperor isn't wearing any clothes!" The child opens the people's eyes to their own foolishness. With these simple words, he takes power over everyone present.

> **"Thank God kids never mean well."**
>
> —Lily Tomlin

> **"A truth once seen even by a single mind always ends by imposing itself on the totality of Human Consciousness."**
>
> —Pierre Teilhard de Chardin

POWER AND EXCUSES

Put yourself in the crowd watching the Emperor go by. Will you speak out honestly, like the child? Will you raise your eyebrows, consider the situation, look around at the other bystanders, and wait for someone else to speak first? Or will you make excuses? ("I'm not wearing my glasses, so I can't really see...what do YOU think of the Emperor's new clothes?")

Excuses can be power-enriching or power-robbing, depending on whether you're making them or taking them. The excuse-maker says, "Please like me; I need your approval." Powerful people don't have to make excuses to less powerful people. The student who is late to class is expected to make excuses; the teacher who is late to class doesn't have to say a word.

The little boy could tell the truth because he didn't care about power. He didn't wonder if other people would think he was foolish. He didn't stop to think that they might disapprove of him.

Most young children are like the boy in the story. They speak the truth as they see it, without thinking about how they will look, how other people will feel, or whether other people will judge them.

Maybe you've been in line behind a parent and child when the child suddenly blurts out, "Lady, you're ugly," or "Mister, why do you only have one leg?" The parent rushes to quiet the child. If the parent scolds the child, the child may protest loudly, "But, Dad, you told me to tell the truth!"

As we get older, we learn to monitor our own behaviors and words, as if we were outside critics. We begin to judge ourselves and others, and we become more aware that others are judging us. Truth gives way to social lies. Raw truth from one adult to another becomes rare. The most likely place you'll find it is in a hospital emergency room. Perhaps that's why some adults choose emergency-room work.

Gossip is another type of power-giving lie. When you talk about other people's mistakes and problems, you feel wise and happy by comparison. After all, *you* would never make those mistakes or get yourself into those terrible situations!

It would have been fun to hear the gossip after the Emperor's parade. You can probably imagine what the people were saying. "I knew the truth all along"..."If the Emperor had asked *me*, I would have told him"..."Our poor Emperor! How will he ever show his face in the village again?"..."That Emperor. What a fool."

"But if everyone can speak the truth to you, then you lose respect."

—Machiavelli

COULD YOU LIVE IN A TRUTHFUL WORLD?

What would it be like to live in a totally truthful world? In a play called "Nothing But the Truth" by James Montgomery, a character accepts a $10,000 bet that he will tell the absolute truth for 24 hours without losing any friends or business associates. It sounds easy, but could you do it?

Your day might begin with someone saying to you, "Good morning, how are you?" What if you don't think the morning is all that good, or you aren't awake enough to have decided, or you don't feel "fine"? You'll lose the bet the moment you say, "Good morning; I'm fine." You can't even ask the other person, "How are you?" unless you really want to know.

So far you've risked two social lies, and you haven't even had breakfast! The next 23 1/2 hours will be very hard indeed.

There are some people who insist on total honesty at all times. They say things like, "Don't take offense, but...," and then they offend you. Or they ask, "Can I be completely honest with you?" Think twice before you answer! People like this may be using the guise of "total honesty" to hurt your feelings or put you down. Sometimes honesty isn't the best policy.

- Another vote against total honesty comes from Japan's medical professionals. In the United States, a dying patient is usually told how long he or she has to live. In Japan, doctors never inform their patients that they are going to die. Which would you prefer?

- A third vote against total honesty comes from certain psychiatrists who believe that they learn more about their patients from the lies they tell than the truths they confess.

How would *you* vote?

> **"A truth that's told with bad intent Beats all the lies you can invent."**
>
> —William Blake

> **"Anything that begins, 'I don't know how to tell you this,' is never good news."**
>
> —Ruth Gordon

CHANGING THE RULES

Lies of convenience, protective lies, and cover-up lies help you to appear polite, intelligent, caring, and worthy of approval. These social lies have become so widespread that you probably don't even think of them as real "lies." That's why you'd be shocked to hear a conversation like this one:

First Tennis Player: "I could have played a better game, but my racket needs to be restrung."

Second Tennis Player (seriously): "You're a liar."

Only when you decide how much approval and acceptance you need, who you need it from, what you're willing to do to get it, and how "perfect" you want to appear, will you know how you really feel about social lies.

If you find them too uncomfortable, you may want to limit your circle of friends to people you can be more truthful with. Or you may choose to play the social game better than everybody else.

Author Robert Fulghum opted to change the rules. He noticed that when adults meet for the first time, they almost always ask each other, "What do you do?" The more he thought about this, the more it seemed to him that when people answer this question by giving their occupation, they are telling only part of the truth.

Fulghum reasoned that what you "do" involves more than what you are paid to do. You sing, you eat, you dance...these are all things you do. Why not answer with one of these non-paid activities?

Since Fulghum spends a lot of time on airplanes, he has been asked "What do you do?" often enough to be bored. One day when a fellow passenger popped the question, Fulghum told her that he was a janitor. He thought his little lie would make his work sound dull, and he wouldn't have to describe what he really did for a living.

To Fulghum's surprise, the woman was fascinated with his answer. It turned out that she was a columnist who wrote about household hints. Fulghum learned a lot about housecleaning that day.

Another time, he answered the question by saying that he was a neurosurgeon. The other passenger replied excitedly, "So am I!"

Now Fulghum has his own in-flight game, which he explains to anyone sitting next to him. They each pick an occupation and pretend for the entire flight that this is what they "do."

Fulghum found a creative way to deal with a social custom he didn't like. So can you. Is there a social custom you're fed up with? Invent an alternative.

TO CONFORM, OR NOT TO CONFORM?

You already know that other people are more likely to approve of you if you dress and act the way they do. If you need a lot of approval, you probably do a lot of conforming.

The interesting thing about conforming is that there are so many different ways to conform! It all depends on which group—or groups—you want to fit into. Do your friends wear Lees or no-label jeans? Earrings in their ears, or in their noses? Champion sweatshirts or army fatigues? Is it cool to show school spirit, or to act like you're bored? Does your group run the school newspaper, power the track team, or drive around in cars with fake-fur seatcovers? If you want to belong, you'll probably conform. Or maybe you're the one who sets the trends.

Even convicted criminals have dress codes and behavior codes within their group—and there are groups within groups. Prisoners who have committed certain types of crimes are not accepted by those who have committed other types of crimes.

The possibilities for conforming are endless, and the rules are amazingly detailed. For example, the executives in one company may *never* wear black raincoats, while the executives in another company may *always* wear them. A suit-and-tie may be required in a bank but look silly in a small architectural firm.

Where you live, the kind of car you drive, the movies you go to see, the books you read, even the food you eat may define you as a member of a certain group in a certain town or city.

The United States is frequently described as a "classless" society, but is it really? Picture an "upper-class person" in your mind. Now picture a "middle-class person." Now picture a "lower-class person." Picture a white-collar worker, and a blue-collar worker. Picture the president of a major corporation, and the president of a labor union. Do specific images come to mind? Those images may be stereotypes—and they may be completely wrong—but they tell you something about conforming and fitting in.

There are so many groups with so many rules that you may wonder how you can possibly win everyone's approval. The answer is: you can't, so don't even try. All you can do is choose your corner and learn the rules that apply there. Or, if you're the independent type, you can forget about conforming and remind yourself that "being like everybody else" doesn't equal "being normal," even if some people say it does.

GOING ALONG WITH THE CROWD

Think about the last time you were in a crowd of people—maybe watching a movie or a basketball game at your school. Did you model your actions on the behavior of the crowd? Did you applaud when others applauded, even if you didn't feel like it?

Did you stand when they stood, and sit when they sat? Did you do the Wave when it came your way? The desire to be "one of the crowd" is a powerful force, like magnetism or electricity.

Have you ever stood up and cheered all alone? (Probably not—too scary!) What if you're the only person who thinks something is funny? Do you laugh out loud or chuckle quietly to yourself?

Even when you conform to a crowd, you still have room to be unique. You applaud when they do, but maybe you do it differently, slapping your right hand on your left or moving both hands back and forth. You sit when they sit, but maybe you're straight and tall instead of slumped, or you're the only one in your row who crosses your legs.

The next time you're in a crowd, look around. You'll see people doing similar things, but in their own ways. The point is, even if you become the most conforming of conformists, you won't be able to imitate everything that other people do. Like it or not, you're unique.

"General notions are generally wrong."

—Lady Mary Wortley Montague

THE TRUTH ABOUT PEER PRESSURE

Who cares if you applaud one way or another? Probably nobody. But your behaviors are important to the people around you, and there will always be those who will try to sell you on their brand of the truth.

Some people call this peer pressure, but it's more accurate to think of it as selling. Is there really any difference between a friend talking you into *doing* something you don't want, and a stranger talking you into *buying* something you don't want? You decide.

Imagine that you're in a crowd applauding your favorite rock star. Your friend turns to you and says, "Why don't you applaud the same way I do?" You might ask, "What's it to you?" Or you might not. Because it's socially more acceptable to go along and get along, you may choose to conform rather than confront your friend.

You may worry that you'll lose your friend's approval if you challenge him. It's true; you may. Or you may find, like the child in "The Emperor's New Clothes," that asking "why" points to the truth and strengthens your position.

There are two kinds of friends: *true friends* and *false friends*. True friends encourage you to do and be your best, and celebrate with you when you're a winner. True friends like you for yourself, and therefore, logically, encourage you to be yourself. They don't like you for what you have or what you can do for them.

True friends respect your right to choose what's best for you. They don't need you to be their follower, and they don't need to follow you. The so-called "friends" who try to change you aren't your true friends. They are using you to satisfy their need to control other people.

> ## TRUTH #4:
> ## IF YOU LIKE YOURSELF MORE AFTER
> ## SPENDING TIME WITH SOMEONE,
> ## HE OR SHE IS A TRUE FRIEND.
> ## IF YOU LIKE YOURSELF LESS,
> ## HE OR SHE IS NOT A TRUE FRIEND.

Before you give in to peer pressure, stop and say, "Wait a minute while I think this over." The same logic you use to weigh the truth will come in handy here.

Ask yourself simple questions like, "What might this lead to?" "Could I get in too deep?" "Am I the one making this decision, or is someone selling it to me?" "Would I advise someone else to do what I'm thinking about doing?" If the answer to this final question is "no," proceed with caution!

When you let another person talk you into something you shouldn't do, you're lying to yourself and blaming him or her. It's ugly, but it's the truth.

GANGS

A gang is a special kind of peer-pressure group. It is organized, like a club, and has its own rules.

Young people join gangs for many different reasons. Here are a few of the most common:

- to feel safer; for protection
- to feel more powerful as part of a group
- to be social and have a group to do things with
- to do mischief without taking all of the blame
- for excitement
- for acceptance.

Here are some of the ways gangs encourage new members to join:

- scare tactics
- dare tactics
- flattery
- guilt
- "everyone does it"
- "it will improve you"
- "it's fun"
- "you need it"
- "it's economical; you'll make money"
- "you'll feel good"
- "you deserve it"
- "only the best people get in."

Usually we perceive gangs as negative. But if we broaden our definition, we can begin to include good "gangs," too. What about a consumer group that protects your interests? What about a neighborhood group that forms to help elderly people in the area?

FORM YOUR OWN GANG

If you could form a gang or club for a positive purpose, what would it be like? Brainstorm some ideas with your friends.

Purpose

What purpose would it have?

Members

Who would be allowed in? Who wouldn't? What would the membership requirements be? What could get you kicked out?

Dress Code

What would members be expected to wear? Would there be a strict dress code?

Colors, etc.

What colors, symbols, signs, and signals would you use?

Language

What new slang words would you invent?

Music

What music would you listen to?

Club Rules

What would your club rules be?

THE TRUTH ABOUT GIFT-GIVING

Gift-giving is another area of life that requires polite social lies. Here again, only children are totally truthful. Only children can open a gift and wail with disappointment without worrying about hurting somebody's feelings. They haven't yet learned to *pretend* to like gifts.

Compare this to the joy parents express over a crude gift their child makes for them in kindergarten. What if instead they were totally honest and said, "Honey, this is a really useless and ugly gift you have made for us, but we'll treasure it forever anyway, because you made it with your own little hands"?

What do you say when you open a gift you don't like? What if it's something you already have? You might hear yourself saying, "This is what I always wanted! I love it! Thanks!" Although this seems like a harmless social lie, it makes real thanks less meaningful. And if you pretend too hard—if you're too enthusiastic about a gift you don't like—you can expect to receive similar gifts in the future.

GIFTS GIVEN, GIFTS RECEIVED

1. What was the BEST gift you ever received? Why?

2. What was the WORST gift you ever received? Why?

3. Did you ever receive a gift you didn't like at the time, but later it became very special to you? What and why?

4. What was the BEST gift you ever gave? How did you know?

5. What was the WORST gift you ever gave? How did you know?

6. What was the MOST INAPPROPRIATE (wrong-for-you) gift you ever received?

Think about it: Is the most expensive gift always the BEST gift? Is the least expensive gift always the WORST gift?

As you get older, you start to realize that gifts aren't just "things." They reveal what your friends and family think of you, and something of how they feel about you. This is what makes gift-giving so emotional and so tricky.

Imagine that you give a friend a pound of licorice for her birthday. You love licorice, but somewhere along the way you have forgotten that your friend *hates* it. There are many ways she might "read" your gift.

- She may think, "You know I hate licorice, and you're just trying to annoy me." Or,

- "If you had thought about my gift, instead of rushing out to buy any old thing, you would have remembered that I hate licorice." Or,

- "You probably just forgot that I hate licorice. It was an innocent mistake. No big deal."

In any case, the licorice is loaded with meaning, intentional or not.

The ritual of exchanging gifts can become more important than the gifts themselves. The occasion, how the gift is wrapped, and what it shows about the giver's knowledge of the receiver's interests are all part of the ritual. For example, most of us don't mind getting money as a gift, if we can spend it however we want. But should a girl give her boyfriend money for Valentine's Day? Probably not. Will a thousand dollars from a millionaire friend have the same meaning as a hand-made quilt from your grandmother? Again, probably not. Your friend is so wealthy that the thousand dollars is a trifle. The quilt has far more significance. It's a unique, one-of-a-kind symbol of your grandmother's time and love.

Gifts also come with obligations—the expectation that we will say or do something in return. A gift presented casually, unwrapped, and with the comment, "I just saw this and picked it up for you," carries less obligation than if the same gift were elaborately wrapped and presented formally in front of an audience.

Gift-giving involves so many different shades of meaning that it's almost impossible to sort them all out. So most of us just smile politely and say "Thank you" when we're thrilled with a gift...and when we're not.

Advertisers use our confusion about gift-giving to trick us into buying their products. We're conditioned to believe that if we get a gift, we must give a gift. This is called the *norm of reciprocity*. Advertisers know that they can send us a small, basically worthless item (an ounce of shampoo, a tiny packet of cookies), and we'll feel obligated to buy something.

A CHRISTMAS MEMORY

by Dan Barnhart

Sometimes a gift leaves a lasting impression because of its deeper meaning. Dan Barnhart is a professional actor and musician, and it has been many years since the incident he describes here, but he still recalls the meaning of one particular gift and what it said about him, to him, and how it changed the "truth" forever.

When I was 7 or 8, I discovered the truth about Santa Claus...well, at least one version of the truth—my Mom's. What had happened was that Santa had made a "mistake" and put my name on a package intended for my brother. So excited was I at Santa's astuteness in giving me a Hardy Boys novel that I had failed to notice my older brother's crestfallen face at the inferior, childish book Santa had chosen for him.

Haven't we all opened that gift that thoroughly surprised and delighted us because we hadn't known that we needed or wanted it? Well, just when I was mentally thanking God and Santa and whomever else I could think of, my Mom said: "Dan, come into the kitchen with me."

It was such a true and honest excitement for me—this book already the greatest of my all-time gifts. It signaled a passage for me—an adultness. A *real* hard bound novel. A sense of the wonderful was upon me and as I began to tell all this to Mom, she said: "That was supposed to be Tim's book."

I stopped dead for a moment, stupefied, blank. "What do you mean?"

"It should have had Tim's name on it."

My mother then proceeded to tell me her version of the truth about you-know-who. "Surely I had suspected." (I hadn't.) "I was getting kind of old anyway. She would have to tell me soon." (I don't think so.) "It was just a mistake." (It was murder.)

A kind of pall and dinginess settled over me like soot. What was dead was more than just a man. It was an idea, a magical sense of infinite possibilities, of innocent acceptance that began to leave me. I wanted to run and scream and deny the horrors of what I had heard. Instead, I willed myself back into the living room, mute and with a feeling of dread. There was a tightness in my throat and my ears were ringing. As each gift was unwrapped, I watched with growing cynicism and saw—not a wonderful surprise—but calculated, foregone conclusions.

The world I knew had changed.

A BRIDGE OF EXCUSES

From admiring an Emperor's nonexistent new clothes to saying thanks for a tacky gift, from making excuses for being late to politely ignoring a friend's big zits, we are all expert social liars.

Our society accepts that the world is emotionally safer when we have a more-or-less organized system for being less than truthful about certain things. Most of our social lies are obvious, but we pretend to believe them anyway.

Maybe we should set aside one day out of the year when we don't have to fake it, apologize, or make excuses. We could call it "National Inappropriate Behavior Day." On this day, if you wore the "wrong" clothes, said the "wrong" thing, were too early, too late, or rude, nobody would raise their eyebrows. Instead, they would shrug their shoulders and say, "It's okay. It is National Inappropriate Behavior Day!"

Vaclav Havel, past president of Czechoslovakia and one of his country's most famous writers, once observed that culture gives us a "bridge of excuses" for choosing not to live within the truth. Some of these excuses are helpful, some are hurtful. Almost all depend on their context—the circumstances that surround them.

There is no "one size fits all" rule. A lie can be kind; a truth can be cruel. Or a lie may work in the short run, but not in the long run.

You will often be called upon to weigh the value of lies your culture considers acceptable. For each, you will need to consider the circumstances, the possible consequences, and the lie itself. It won't be easy to decide what's right for you, but keep on trying.

CHAPTER 5

MYTH-MATICS

Sam travels from New York City to Los Angeles to meet his friend, Clu. First, Sam needs to find out what gang Clu belongs to.

There are three gangs:
- the Fats, who always tell the truth,
- the Skinnies, who always lie, and
- the Muscles, who sometimes lie and sometimes tell the truth.

Sam meets three people, one from each gang. He asks each of them two questions:
1. "What gang do you belong to?"
2. "What gang does my friend, Clu, belong to?"

Targa (#1) says, "I am not a Fat. Clu is a Skinny."
Braun (#2) says, "I am not a Skinny. Clu is a Muscle."
String (#3) says, "I am not a Muscle. Clu is a Fat."

Can you figure out what gangs Targa, Braun, and String belong to? Can you identify Clu's gang from the information they gave Sam?

Find the answers on page **154**.

THE TRUTH ABOUT MATH

Three cheers for math! You can always count on it. The logic of math helps you solve puzzles, like the one about Sam and Clu. We love numbers because they make opinions sound so right, so absolute—just like facts. Numbers are music to our ears.

Numbers don't lie, right? And neither do the people who work miracles with them...right?

Imagine that two people offer to check your math homework for you. One is a college student, and the other is the great mathematician, Sir Isaac Newton. Which will you choose?

If you pick Sir Isaac, you might be sorry later...much later.

In the 1980's, a University of Chicago student named Robert Garisto found a mistake in the master scientist's calculations. Sir Isaac Newton had made a rather obvious mathematical error about 300 years ago, but because he was an "expert," nobody bothered to look for it. People often accept an expert's word as fact.

When the Emperor didn't question the "expert" cloth salesmen, he made a big mistake. So did Dorothy when she didn't ask the Wizard how he planned to send her back to Kansas. When you trust "authorities" and "experts" to give you honest information, you are asking to be misled.

If you want numbers to tell you the truth, follow this rule:

Check, doublecheck, ask questions,
and be tough-minded
even if (especially if) the person with the numbers
is an "authority" or an "expert."

Numbers aren't just answers; they are also questions. For example, "four" is the answer to the problem, "What's two plus two?" But it is also the question, "What else can result in four?"

. . . .

FOUR POOR REASONS TO BELIEVE SOMETHING

1. **"We've believed it for a long time!"**
2. **"So many people believe it!"**
3. **"A famous person said so!"**
4. **"ONE astounding example! That proves it!"**

. . . .

MATH SCAMS

- Until 1989, an American cereal came in a box that measured
  9 1/4" x 6 5/8" x 2 1/8" and contained 12 ounces of cereal.

  In 1989, the company introduced a new box. It measured
  1 3/8" higher and contained 12.2 ounces of cereal.

  The volume of the box grew almost 15 percent; the amount of
  cereal increased by less than 2 percent. Printed across the front
  of the box were the words, "New Larger Size."

- A car dealer in Illinois advertised a "1/2 PRICE SALE" in giant
  letters. The second line, in much smaller letters, read, "The
  price you see is half the price you pay."

- A Canadian company invited Lotto players to join a "Winners
  Club." Instead of playing Lotto alone, club members would
  play in a group of 200. Each group was guaranteed to win
  at least $1,250.

  Divide $1,250 by 200, and you get $6.25—each member's
  guaranteed minimum winnings share.

  Joining the Winners Club cost $29.95 plus $2 postage
  and handling.

WHEN NUMBERS LIE

You'll probably get good grades in math if you memorize
math facts. But you need more than a head full of facts to truly
understand numbers. To grasp all the statistics thrown at you
every day in polls, charts, speeches, and advertising, you need
to know how real people use numbers in the real world.

The same set of numbers can be used in different ways to
influence your thinking, beliefs, and behavior. That's why you
need to find out who is reporting them and what they have
to gain.

For example, if you read a study which "proves" that
cigarette smoking is healthful, you will want to learn who did
the study (doctors? scientists?) and who paid for it (a tobacco
company? the Lung Association?). The answers will help you
decide how much you can trust what you read.

MYTH-MATICS

"Figures won't lie, but
liars will figure."

—Charles H. Grosvenor

Dear Dr. Science: "If you
add two even numbers,
you get an even number.
If you add two odd
numbers, you get an even
number. The only way to
get an odd number is to
add an even number and
an odd number. So why
aren't there twice as
many odd numbers?"

Dr. Science: "Get a life!"

—"Ask Dr. Science"

Numbers lie when you let them—when you don't take time to learn the language of math, or when you overlook obvious errors, or when you don't ask questions. How did Newton's mistake go undiscovered for 300 years? Perhaps because for centuries people thought, "Who am I to question an expert?"

You may have heard illogical-sounding statements which "felt" wrong but turned out to be right. As a result, you may hesitate to speak up when something seems wrong to you.

You may have heard logical-sounding statements which "felt" right but turned out to be wrong. It's hard to question something that seems right.

But if you don't question what seems wrong and you don't question what seems right, you may not question anything. You'll accept at face value whatever numbers come your way.

It's easier to think, "Gee, isn't that strange?" than to challenge the figures. You're more likely to doubt yourself than to question numbers which dazzle you by appearing to be "facts." It's easy to forget that behind every set of numbers is a human being who may be arranging the numbers to make an impression...or who may be mistaken.

You may be so used to our illogical world that illogical events, comments, and numbers don't stand out. Consider the story about the man who saved pieces of string. After he died, his granddaughter found a box in his basement labeled, "PIECES OF STRING TOO SMALL TO SAVE."

We all do and say equally silly things. Baseball player Yogi Berra was famous for remarks like, "Nobody goes there anymore; it's too crowded." In its own way, this completely illogical statement makes "sense."

Someone once asked Yogi, "Would you like your pizza cut in four or eight slices?" Yogi replied, "Four. I don't think I can eat eight."

What about when...

...someone calls a radio talk show to proclaim, "This topic isn't important enough to be discussed on your program"?

...someone makes a toll call to an opinion poll, just to register an opinion of "undecided"?

...someone says, "I can't decide whether or not I'm 100% sure about that"?

On any day, you can find plenty of examples of illogical thinking and behavior. Scan the newspaper and you're bound to read something that makes no sense. Or listen to conversations, and you'll overhear morsels of foolishness—as in "Can I ask you a question?" or "Are you asleep?"

THE TROUBLE WITH SHOULDS

A law requiring people to wear seat belts *should* lower the fatality rate from automobile accidents. It not only *seems* right; we *want* it to be right. So when we read, "Traffic fatalities have gone down 10% since the new seat belt law took effect," we accept this as "proof" that seat belt laws save lives.

They probably do, but the statistic by itself is not proof.

We often accept as "true" anything that seems as if it "should be true." Remember that a number is both an answer and a question. What else happened around the same time the seat belt law was passed? Were the roads improved? Was the speed limit changed? Did more people start riding the bus instead of driving to work?

When you accept the "10% reduction" statistic without asking questions, you're jumping to conclusions. When you make decisions based on these conclusions, you're asking for trouble.

- If you read a magazine article stating that you're more likely to survive a car accident at 7 a.m. than at 7 p.m. because "four times more people are killed on the highways at 7 p.m. than at 7 a.m.," what will you do?

  Will you avoid driving at 7 p.m.? Or will you realize that more people are on the highways at 7 p.m., so it's reasonable to expect that more will be involved in accidents at that time of day?

- If you read an article reporting that "75% of crimes are committed by Canadians," what will you think?

  Will you immediately conclude that Canadians are bad people? Or will you reason that the statistic probably applies only to Canada, where Canadians do commit most of the crimes—not because they're bad people, but because they're in the majority?

What statistics have you accepted just because they sounded logical, or because you wanted to believe them? Have you ever been fooled by "shoulds"?

STUDIES SHOW....

Many of our behaviors and decisions are based on reports which begin with these two powerful words, "Studies show...."

But before you buy that new acne remedy, take the time to ask a few questions about those "studies that show."

1. **Studies show that rice bran lowers blood cholesterol. Therefore, you should...**

   A. start eating rice bran every morning

   B. find out who the subjects of the experiments were

2. **Studies show that three out of five people prefer Brand A over Brand B. Therefore, you should...**

   A. start buying Brand A

   B. ask how many people took part in the study

3. **A recent study of oat bran showed that it is good for you. Therefore, you should...**

   A. ask who paid for the study

   B. eat oat bran

4. **Studies show that people who had difficult childhoods ate white bread. Therefore you should...**

   A. avoid white bread

   B. find out if this study was *retrospective*—based on what subjects remembered

5. **Studies show that people who jog five miles a day look younger. Therefore you should...**

   A. jog five miles a day

   B. find out how the subjects were chosen

Find the answers on page **155**.

THE POWER OF STATISTICS

The branch of mathematics known as *statistics* was originally invented for government purposes. When tribes united to form nations, rulers needed to know how many men were available to fight, how many children there were to feed, how much wealth existed in the group, how much tax money could be collected, and so on. Statistics gave them a way to collect, analyze, interpret, and manipulate these numbers.

Today we're deluged with statistics in the form of percentages, polls, surveys, rates, charts, and graphs. Statistics influence the way we think, vote, and spend our money.

We know that statistics are sometimes used to mislead us or even lie to us. But they are still numbers, and numbers have power. So we give statistics the benefit of the doubt, and we let them shape our opinions and our decisions.

You often hear statistics used to compare events from different years or decades. Someone will claim that the state of the economy is 20% better or worse than it was ten years ago, or that unemployment is up or down 5% from last year.

The numbers themselves may be true. They are just not the whole story. You are hearing half-truths.

For example, during the 1980's, the U.S. government changed the way it collected unemployment figures. It also changed the way it defined the word "unemployment." Few people were aware of either change.

The government used to count people as unemployed if they were out of work, and employed if they were working. Those in the military were not counted among the employed.

Then someone decided that military personnel were indeed "employed" and should be included in those statistics. You can imagine how this affected the unemployment figures. Suddenly millions of people were moved from the "unemployed" column to the "employed" column. Almost overnight, the unemployment rate fell. It looked as if more people were employed.

Unemployment figures were changed in another important way. People who had been out of work for so long that they couldn't collect unemployment compensation anymore were dropped from the "unemployed" count. They were still out of work, but according to the government, they were no longer unemployed. Once again, the unemployment rate fell.

You can't compare unemployment rates from year to year, not when they are figured in such different ways. Or, rather, you *can* compare them, but your comparisons won't have any real meaning. They may be useful for impressive-sounding speeches, but not much else. The rates add up to a half-truth, worthless unless you know how unemployment is defined.

- If a statistic claims that there are more "rich" people this year than last year, get out your lie-detector! How is "rich" being defined? To someone with very little money, "rich" may be anyone with $10,000—an amount the government defines as "poverty level" for a family of three.

"One half-truth equals one whole lie."

—Old Saying

"A man who tells lies like me, merely hides the truth. But a man who tells half-lies has forgotten where he put it."

—Diplomat to Major Lawrence in the movie, "Lawrence of Arabia"

- If you read that "tall people" live longer, heads up! How is "tall" being defined? "Longer" than what? Longer than short people? Longer than fruit flies?

When statistics are used to compare years or decades, you can expect the numbers to be distorted because so many other parts of the "truth" will have changed.

- If you hear that "there is 30% more crime today than there was 10 years ago," take cover! Does "more" mean that people in general have become more unlawful? Or perhaps the population has grown, or more people are reporting crimes, or there are more police officers to catch criminals.

- If you learn that "income has increased by 25% from 10 years ago," hold on to your wallet! Whose income has increased? Does this figure include any changes in the cost of living? If you get a raise, but the cost of food rises even faster, you may end up with less money in your pocket than before you started earning more.

Statistics can lead you astray by telling you stories in numbers too large or too small for you to comprehend. This is comparable to you telling a four-year-old a fairy tale in seven-syllable words. The whole message is lost.

The numbers you hear most often in statistics are in the millions and billions and trillions. How can you get a grasp on figures this size? **TIP:** Translate big numbers into units that are easier for you to imagine. For example, one million seconds equal 12 days; one billion seconds equal 32 years; one trillion seconds equal about 32,000 years.

Now, when you compare one trillion to one million (seconds, dollars, or anything else), at least you can have a reasonably accurate picture in your mind: 32,000 years to 12 days. That puts the U.S. national debt in a whole new light.

Along with their "real" value, numbers have a psychological value that is rarely taken into account. Numbers at the low end of a scale seem bigger than those at the high end of a scale.

A one-year-old and a five-year-old seem much farther apart in age than a 41-year-old and a 45-year-old. The difference between a four-pound infant and a nine-pound infant seems greater than the difference between a 272-pound football player and a 277-pound football player. This psychological value further fuzzies what might seem like an objective numerical report.

SENSELESS STATISTICS

If you come face to face with a statistic, stand your ground and pull out your most wicked questions:

1. "Is this something that *must* be true, or something that *might* be true?"

2. "Is this a fact or an opinion?"

3. "How are the terms defined?"

4. "Who says?"

5. "Who paid for this statistic?"

6. "Who stands to benefit from this statistic?"

7. "What else can you tell me about it?"

8. "Does it make sense?"

One day you open your mailbox to find a letter asking for donations. The letter reads:

Help save the extremely rare Moolaboola fly! This precious natural resource is dying out at a rate of a million a day, and there are only 10 million left on Earth....Your $25 can make the difference between life and extinction!

What's wrong with these statistics? They don't make sense! If a million Moolaboolas are dying each day, then it will take only 10 days for the species to become extinct—long before the letter can be written, printed, mailed, and read by you, and long before you can send your $25 to a lost cause.

> **"There are three kinds of lies: lies, damned lies, and statistics."**
>
> —Benjamin Disraeli

> **"I always find that statistics are hard to swallow and impossible to digest. The only one I can ever remember is that if all the people who go to sleep in church were laid end to end they would be a lot more comfortable."**
>
> —Martha Wheaton Bowers Taft

BELIEVE IT OR NOT

Consider the following statistics. Ask questions about each one and think about how much truth it contains. What, if anything, is missing from the information provided?

1. The U.S. government says that there are 8.3 million jobless people. The AFL-CIO, a trade union, says that a more realistic figure is 15.4 million, which includes "discouraged and part-time workers who want to be full-time workers."

2. *Dollars and Sense* magazine reports that during the 1980's, 2.2 million more children became poor. If this trend continues, we will have 14.8 children living in poverty by the year 2000.

3. *Christian Science Monitor* reports that the median income of a young family with parents aged 25-34 declined in constant 1989 dollars from $31,544 in 1971 to $30,873 in 1989.

4. Figures from the U.S. Commerce Department show that the welfare rolls are at their highest level in history. Some 4.4 million families receive Aid for Dependent Children (AFDC). Over 23 million individuals receive food stamps.

5. In 1940, corporations paid 57% of the national income tax and individuals paid 43%. In 1985, corporations paid 15% and individuals paid 85%.

HOW TO USE NUMBERS TO PROVE ALMOST ANYTHING

If numbers didn't have to make sense, you could use them to prove almost anything. For example, here's how to use numbers to prove that you don't go to school.

1. There are 365 days in a year, and 1/3 of your life is spent in bed, so that adds up to about 122 days off of your year.

2. You spend 3 hours per day eating—45 more days down the drain.

3. Take away 90 summer vacation days and 21 more miscellaneous holidays (Christmas, spring break, etc.). Total: 111 more days.

4. There are 52 Saturdays and 52 Sundays without school—another 104 days.

Now add your non-school days together: 122 + 45 + 111 + 104 = 382, or 17 *more* than 365, the actual number of days in a year.

THE LAW OF AVERAGES

When you hear a sports announcer give an athlete's "average" score, how do you understand it? Do you think you are hearing the figure that results from adding all the individual scores together and then dividing by their number?

If so, you are thinking of the *mean*. The mean is only one type of average, but it is the one the "average" person usually thinks of first.

The word "average" may also refer to the *median* or the *mode*, which are calculated in completely different ways.

- The *mean* is actually a quotient. For example, a basketball player scores 26, 12, 8, 8, 40, 0, and 32 points in seven games. 26 + 12 + 8 + 8 + 40 + 0 + 32 = 126 divided by 7 equals her *mean* score: 18.

- The *median* is the number exactly in the middle, with as many above it as below it. Putting the basketball player's scores in ascending order—0, 8, 8, 12, 26, 32, 40—we find that her *median* score is 12.

- The *mode* is just the number that shows up most often; in this case, 8.

So we have three numbers—18, 12, and 8. Which one represents the player's average score?

> **"Then there is the man who drowned crossing a stream with an average depth of six inches."**
>
> —W.I.E. Gates

SHOULD YOU TAKE THIS JOB, OR SHOVE IT?

You have a job interview with Company X. The personnel manager tells you that the average salary at the company is $10,000 a year. That sounds okay...until you decide to attend a stockholders' meeting. (Stockholders are people who own shares in a company.)

At the meeting, you hear the president tell the stockholders, "We're really saving money on salaries, because our average salary is only $500 a year!"

Suddenly suspicious, you decide to find out more. You call the company and pretend to be writing an article for your local newspaper. You casually ask, "What's the average salary at Company X?" The company spokesperson answers, "$1,000 a year."

Who is telling the truth—the personnel manager, the president, or the company spokesperson? You decide. Here's a list of the salaries paid out by the company:

1. $45,000 per year to the president of the company

2. $3,000 per year to the vice-president of the company

3. $1,000 per year to the manager

4. $500 per year to Worker #1

5. $500 per year to Worker #2.

Find the answers on pages **155-156**.

POLL PROBLEMS

Most statistics you read and hear can be dismissed as relatively meaningless. The same goes for polls.

You can hardly get through a day without hearing the results of one poll or another, especially during an election year. Many people follow this simple rule when it comes to polls: They agree with those that express their opinion, and they don't agree with those that don't express their opinion.

Actually, this is a perfectly sensible rule where polls are concerned. It is about as close as you can get to knowing the truth of most polls presented as "news."

Polls are influenced by so many variables that it's amazing we take them seriously. Some of these variables include...

...how the question is asked

Compare "In your opinion, is it okay to smoke while you pray?" to "In your opinion, is it okay to pray while you smoke?"

...who asks the question

The question is, "Have you ever driven while intoxicated?" Does it matter if the question is asked by a) a college student or b) a police officer?

...when the question is asked

Questions asked in the summer might get more optimistic answers than questions asked in the dead of winter.

...who the respondents are

The question is, "Do you like bubble gum?" Does it matter if the respondents are a) 8-year-olds or b) 80-year-olds?

...how the respondents are selected

A telephone poll conducted in the afternoon selects only those respondents who a) have telephones and b) are at home in the afternoon.

"Fifty million Frenchmen can't be wrong."

—Texas Guinan

"If 1,000 people say a foolish thing, it is still a foolish thing."

—Old Chinese saying

"Accurate knowledge is the basis of correct opinion; the want of it makes the opinion of many people of little value."

—Alexander Pope

...whether the respondents tell the truth

Polls are often wrong because people lie to the pollsters. They want to give "pleasing" answers that make them "look good."

...and on and on.

Can you think of other variables?

What is the real purpose of so many polls? Are we supposed to use them to check the "correctness" of our own opinions? In the end, who cares what other people say, or think, or say they think? The answer to that question is...we all do.

We buy one brand of aspirin instead of another because 9 out of 10 doctors recommend it. When 80% of all teenagers polled say they like a certain brand of jeans, the other 20% want some, too. When the President's approval rating drops by 14 percentage points, it's time to schedule some baby-kissing public appearances. Polls have great influence in our lives...more than we may realize.

GEORGE GALLUP, POLLSTER EXTRAORDINAIRE

If you pay attention to polls, you have heard people refer to something called the "Gallup Poll."

George Gallup was hired in 1922 by the *St. Louis Post-Dispatch* to question every reader about the newspaper's contents. Six years later, he earned a Ph.D. His thesis was that an accurate poll could be taken from a small number of people, *if* the people polled were selected in a very careful, scientific way he had designed. His methods saved time and effort, made polls more practical, and brought them into wider use.

Gallup became well-known nationally when his polls correctly predicted presidential election results. He wasn't always right; like many pollsters, he wrongly predicted that Harry Truman would lose the 1948 election. But he didn't let his mistakes bother him. Instead, he bragged, "I could prove God statistically."

MORE NUMBER POINTERS

- Newspapers and TV news programs are full of graphs and charts. Read them with a critical eye. Never trust a graph or chart without numbers—and question the numbers you see.

- It's generally accepted that if you ask people their age or weight, they don't have to tell you the truth. (Plus asking is often considered rude.) In France, a middle-aged woman is referred to as a woman *d'un certain âge* (of a certain age). A woman in France only has to count her age up to 40!

- If you ever sign a contract, be sure to give all the numbers on it your own special lie-detector test. And *read the small print.*

  For example, you decide to purchase a new stereo system for $1,000, and you agree to pay $40 per month. It would seem that your stereo would be paid for in 25 months, or just over 2 years.

  Wrong! When you buy something on credit, you also agree to pay interest—a monthly "finance charge." Finance charges add up fast. You will pay more for your stereo, and you will make payments for longer than 25 months.

- When is a moral belief like a scientific truth? When it comes with numbers and an experiment attached.

  Numbers magically transform opinions and theories into "science." If you disagree with a moral truth, you aren't judged crazy or stupid, because it's your opinion against someone else's. But try disagreeing with a scientific "truth" and see what happens.

"The secret of staying young is to live honestly, eat slowly, and lie about your age."

—Lucille Ball

CRITICAL MASS: SCIENCE OR MYTH?

Some people use science and math to promote ideas and ideals they want others to believe. If you can support your argument with experiments and numbers, few will question your basic concept, even if there is little or no truth to it.

If someone told you about the existence of a "magic number," how would you respond? Would you be skeptical? Would you laugh? What if the person gave the "magic number" a scientific name?

This is what happened with *The Hundredth Monkey*, a book by science writer Lyall Watson. In it, Watson told the story of a female macaque (a type of monkey) on a small Japanese island.

Somehow this macaque, named Imo, learned to wash sweet potatoes before eating them, which no other monkey on the island had ever done. Imo started teaching this skill to her family and friends.

Then one day, according to Watson, the "hundredth monkey" learned the skill. Suddenly all of the macaques on the island knew it, as if the knowledge had passed instantaneously from monkey brain to monkey brain.

Watson picked 100 as the "magical number" at which this phenomenon supposedly occurred. But he didn't call it a "magical number." He called it "critical mass," a scientific-sounding name. Watson's concept was quickly accepted.

The Hundredth Monkey story has more in common with myth than science. In fact, there is a less spectacular—and more scientific—explanation for what happened on Imo's island. The female macaques who had learned potato-washing started having babies. The babies learned the behavior directly from their mothers. Nothing magical there.

But that's not the way many people saw it. They used Watson's story as the basis for other "scientific" ideas. Each new idea moved farther from the truth.

For example, if "critical mass" is true for monkeys, then it must follow that it's true for human beings. Maybe a group of people could spread their ideas throughout the population, reach a "critical mass," and suddenly everyone would share the same "new, enlightened" knowledge.

On the surface, that sounds exciting. Wouldn't it be great if learning were that easy? If ideas could be transmitted instantly? If everyone knew all of the same things, all at the same time?

Think again. Theoretically, you could be sitting somewhere, innocently sipping a milkshake, and suddenly get the urge to join a peace march...or a war rally, depending on the beliefs and goals of the "critical mass."

Writing about Imo in *Omni* magazine, Maureen O'Hara points out that "individuals who think for themselves, make their own choices—people who uphold their convictions even against the majority—are unimportant in this view of social change." If there were such a thing as "critical mass," it would mean the end of independent thought and free choice.

The Hundredth Monkey shows how dangerous it can be to confuse science with myth. Wearing scientific clothing, myths can be passed off as truths, where they go unquestioned and unchallenged. Other ideas are built on these myths and accepted because they, too, seem "scientific." This is the same kind of false science that has been used to "prove" such ideas as women's inferiority and the superiority of the Aryan "race."

But *The Hundredth Monkey* certainly sounded good. It appealed to people who wanted to believe in the "new" concept of critical mass. It was written by a science writer. It was full of scientific language. It even had a number: 100. And because it contained all of the right ingredients, many people believed it, including those who should have known better.

REGRESSION TO THE MEAN

Simple mathematical truths are sometimes used to construct complex scientific theories. For example, psychologists Amos Tversky and Daniel Kahneman did a study of beginning pilots. The pilots were praised after making good landings, and scolded after making bad landings.

Tversky and Kahneman reported that "behavior is most likely to improve after punishment and to deteriorate after reward. Consequently, the human condition is such that...one is most often rewarded for punishing others, and most often punished for rewarding them." From their report, it would be easy to conclude that rewarding good performance is bad, and punishing poor performance is good.

Actually, the pilots' behavior followed a law of *numbers,* not a law of behavior. After a very good performance, the next one tends to be worse, and after a very poor performance, the next one tends to be better. This is called *regression to the mean*. Any extreme, either good or bad, tends to fall back to the average range.

This concept can help you when you're faced with convincing statistics. What if you read that "the economy has improved by 20 percent"? Maybe the "improvement" is just a natural swing back to the mean following a period when the economy *worsened* by 20 percent. Maybe no real improvement has taken place after all.

You can also apply this concept to your own life. What if you follow a string of straight A's with a B in social studies? Maybe that B is a natural swing back to your mean; maybe your "average" performance is a B, while an A represents what you can achieve with extra effort and hard work.

And maybe you need to keep your performance in perspective. Life is a series of ups and downs, and when you get all A's, there's no place to go but down. It's only natural, and it doesn't mean that you're a failure.

COINCIDENCE OR MIRACLE?

Do unusual events stand out in your mind more than ordinary events? For example, if you visited Paris and ran into your next-door neighbor at the Eiffel Tower, would you be amazed by the coincidence? Most people would.

On the other hand, you probably aren't amazed that you exist. But the chances of your existing were one in seven trillion! Your birth was a rare and unusual event, and also a common and usual event, since it happens to everyone.

Albert Einstein once said, "There are two ways to live your life. One is as though nothing is a miracle. The other is as though everything is a miracle." Einstein's knowledge of mathematical language taught him that everything is both ordinary *and* extraordinary.

See for yourself with this simple card experiment.

1. Shuffle a normal deck of cards and deal out 13, face up, one at a time.

2. Write down the order in which the cards came up.

3. Shuffle the cards again and see how long it takes to repeat the same order.

What if your first deal was A/2/3/4/5/6/7/8/9/10/J/Q/K? You would see that as an unusual, even amazing event. But why would it be any more amazing than the 13 cards you actually dealt? That sequence was unusual in its own way, as you soon discovered if you tried to repeat it.

We tend to notice "significant" events, like the A/2/3...J/Q/K deal, while ignoring other events which are equally significant. In the same way, we are impressed by "correct" predictions made by psychics, but we ignore or forget any wrong predictions.

You can make a lot of accurate predictions, simply by making a lot of predictions. The more you predict, the more likely you are to be right.

The A/2/3...J/Q/K deal has special meaning just because we say it does. We could also deal 4/7/5/8/6/9 and call it "amazing" because every other number is consecutive (4/5/6 and 7/8/9).

It all depends on how we see the cards. It's tempting to read meaning into numerical "facts" without "getting the facts"—or even "after the fact."

TRUTH #5:
THE BEST PREDICTOR OF FUTURE BEHAVIOR IS PAST BEHAVIOR.

In experiments where magicians have pretended to be psychic and then admitted to being "fakes," some otherwise intelligent people have kept believing in the magicians' "special powers." They may even twist the truth around to make a wrong prediction "fit."

Many people *want* to believe in the existence of special powers. As psychologist/philosopher William James once said, "We believe as much as we can. We would believe everything if we could."

Numbers can mislead you in many ways. They encourage you to believe in "magic," fool you into paying too much for a product, lead you to accept doubtful "proofs," and convince you that polls are right. But the only way numbers can lie to you is if you let them.

If you learn their language, pay attention, ask questions, and never accept a half-truth as a whole, numbers will stay true to you...most of the time.

CHAPTER 6

THERE ARE NO CATS IN AMERICA

. . . .

TRUE OR FALSE?

About George Washington...
A. He chopped down a cherry tree.
B. He threw a dollar across the Delaware River.
C. His troops at Valley Forge were freezing, starving, and naked.
D. He misspelled the word *lie* "l-y-e."

About Betsy Ross...
E. She stitched the first American flag.
F. She designed the first American flag.
G. Her grandson was a liar.

Find the answers on page **156**.

. . . .

MYTH OR HISTORY?

Each nation has its own history, and each culture has its favorite myths. But did you know that history and myth can be one and the same? Both are used to support the way the people of a culture want to see themselves, and the way they want others to see them. Historical facts are often changed to fit the self-view the culture values.

"There are no cats in America, and the streets are paved with cheese."

—An American Tail

If the Americans had lost the Revolutionary War, there would be no stories about George Washington and his deeds. Americans might still be English subjects who would rather not hear about Washington and his group of rebels.

It's the winners who write the history books. Since all the facts can't be told, the winners usually choose to relate only those facts which make them look heroic, thoughtful, generous, and great. Whether someone is labeled a "freedom fighter" or a "terrorist" depends on who is telling the story.

It would be simple to condemn this practice, and to assume that only the bad guys do it. But we all interpret events in a way that puts us in the best possible light. It's human nature.

An American might speak one minute about the "day of infamy" when Japan bombed Pearl Harbor, and the next minute defend the United States' bombing of Hiroshima. He will cite many facts to support his opinion, which he sees as the truth. Meanwhile, across the ocean, a Japanese citizen might condemn the bombing of Hiroshima while claiming that the attack on Pearl Harbor was justified. He will also have facts to support his opinion, which he sees as the truth.

Americans love stories about democracy, shrewd business sense, thrift, individualism, and bravery. Those are the ideals they value. Other cultures value other ideals, as reflected in their stories. For example, the Chinese admire and respect their elders; the Japanese prize cooperation; Russians value philosophical thought and poetry; the Dutch are fond of maximum freedom.

TRUE OR FALSE?

1. Americans are much taller today than they were in the time of the Revolutionary War.

2. Nobody knows what caused the Civil War.

3. Nobody knows what caused the Great Depression.

4. Many American soldiers have returned home safely from wars because the bullets that hit them were deflected by Bibles they carried in their pockets.

5. The great American fortunes were made by robber barons or people who happened to get lucky at the right time.

6. History is destined to repeat itself.

Find the answers on page **156.**

Think of different cultures, and certain qualities come to mind, such as cleanliness and efficiency. These qualities represent the identity each nation has created for itself—a manufactured truth. To create and spread these cultural illusions, both historical and fictional stories must be popularized and made to seem "real."

Americans didn't want to raise their children on English stories about Robin Hood and King Arthur. They needed new stories to support their new identity as a nation. They gave little thought to the Native Americans and their identity. Like most groups (and individuals), the early Americans thought mainly of themselves.

Here are some American myths you probably already know...except that you learned them as history.

MYTH: The Pilgrims wore black clothes, no jewelry, and funny hats, and they loved democracy.

FACT: They wore bright colors, jewelry, and no funny hats. Most surprising, they did not love democracy. They lived under a sort of "communist" system, in which new settlers were forced to turn over their private supplies for the good of the common welfare.

MYTH: Manhattan was purchased from the Indians in 1626 for only $24.00.

FACT: Manhattan was purchased from the Canarsee Indians, who didn't actually own it (but sold it anyway). The island belonged to the Weckquaesgeeks, who were pretty unhappy with the deal. Eventually they were also paid for Manhattan.

MYTH: Benjamin Franklin was a model of financial responsibility and hard work ("A penny saved is a penny earned....Early to bed and early to rise....").

FACT: Franklin was not especially thrifty, nor was he a workaholic. He was quite a spender who enjoyed his leisure, too.

MYTH: David Henry Thoreau was a rugged individualist and lone woodsman who retreated to the forest of Walden Pond to seek the truth.

FACT: Thoreau wasn't really a loner, and he wasn't much of a woodsman either. (P.S.: Does "David Henry Thoreau" sound funny to you? You probably learned his name as "Henry David Thoreau." But his given name was David Henry. He reversed the order because he thought it sounded better.)

MYTH: Ernest Hemingway was a war hero, wounded in battle.

FACT: Hemingway never actually fought in a war. During World War I, he joined a volunteer ambulance unit in Italy; he was wounded while serving chocolate to the soldiers. He was a foreign correspondent during World War II.

Do democracy-loving Pilgrims in strange hats appeal to you more than communistic pilgrims? Are you more impressed by someone who swindles Indians than someone who gets swindled by them? Do human symbols of thrift, hard work, individualism, and heroism seem less symbolic when you learn that they were only human? If you can truthfully answer "yes" to any of these questions, then you understand how historical myths happen.

BOOTSTRAPS STORIES

Americans like to see themselves as people of a classless society who can achieve anything through hard work. For many years, the Horatio Alger stories were favorites because they promoted this self-view.

Horatio Alger was the oldest child of a Unitarian minister, and he eventually became a minister himself. His books for boys, popular in post-Civil War America, tell of poor lads who get rich through hard work and good character. They "pull themselves up by their bootstraps." Alger's stories helped to spread the American myth that *anyone* could rise up out of poverty simply by working hard and following the rules.

These stories contain more truth than may be obvious at first. In each case, the poor boy gets a lucky break. Americans tend to overlook this part. Instead, they insist that anyone who isn't successful in America has only himself or herself to blame.

On the one hand, the bootstraps myth is good because it encourages self-reliance. On the other, it's frustrating to those who work hard but still don't achieve success. And it's meaningless to those who never have the chance to work hard.

If you investigate stories of people who have "made it on their own," you often find that they had something to start with, or they got lucky. Or they had the sense or training to recognize opportunities which came along—and the chance to take advantage of them.

A successful author once told an audience that she had started with "nothing" and turned it into a million dollars. That, she insisted, qualified her to tell other people what to do with their money. In fact, the author started with a thousand dollars—more than most of us have to play with. She had attended private schools for most of her life, and had graduated from Stanford University.

To many of her listeners, the author's qualifications represented advantages they couldn't even dream of. The author didn't see them that way because she had always enjoyed them. She truly believed that she had started with nothing.

TRUE OR FALSE?

Some myths are used to entertain children and keep them in line. Can you tell which of the following are "guidance myths" and which are truths?

1. Touch toads and you'll get warts.

2. If you cross your eyes, they might get stuck that way.

3. It's dangerous to drink and drive.

4. If you swallow gum, it takes seven years to digest.

5. Smoking is bad for your health.

6. If you go outdoors without a jacket, you'll catch cold.

7. Practice makes perfect.

8. Babies need hugs to stay healthy.

9. Reading in the dark is bad for your eyes.

10. Tomatoes are poisonous.

Find the answers on page **157**.

CHANGING ATTITUDES

Sometimes popular stories come under attack after being told for many years. How can this be true when the stories themselves haven't changed?

Mark Twain's *The Adventures of Huckleberry Finn*, published in 1884, has long been considered one of the greatest works of American fiction. Among its many themes are rugged individualism, adventure, and youth, all part of the American self-image. But in recent years, *Huckleberry Finn* has been criticized for "racism" and "inappropriate language."

What can we learn from this? First, that stories are important for creating a cultural identity. Why would people care about 100-year-old *Huckleberry Finn* if it weren't influential? And second, that cultural identity is a *changing truth*. Otherwise, a book that was acceptable 100 years ago would still be acceptable today, and 100 years from today.

As a culture's self-image changes over time, some old stories are replaced by new ones. Others survive, but not without a fight. Following is a list of books that have taken the rocky ride of changing cultural attitudes. Some people today have very strong objections to these books. Can you figure out why? What is there about each one that some people might find offensive?

- *The Wizard of Oz*
- *Alice in Wonderland*
- *The Chronicles of Narnia*
- *A Wrinkle in Time*
- *Charlie and the Chocolate Factory*
- *Mother Goose: Old Nursery Rhymes*
- *Oliver Twist*
- *Are You There God? It's Me, Margaret*
- *The Adventures of Sherlock Holmes*
- *The Diary of Anne Frank*
- *Webster's Ninth New Collegiate Dictionary.*

ARE YOU OFFENDED?

- The Multicultural Management Program at the University of Missouri School of Journalism has produced a "bad-word dictionary" listing words and phrases some people consider "unacceptable" and "offensive." Their dictionary includes:

— Dutch treat	— senile	— jock
— burly	— stunning	— matronly
— ugh	— airhead	— elderly
— pert	— dear	

  Can you guess why some people might object to these words? Are there any you find "unacceptable" and "offensive"? Do you think that people should be able to use them anyway?

- Many people in the U.S. today are debating whether sports teams should be named "Indians," "Braves," "Chiefs," and "Redskins." Professional teams are slow to respond, but some public schools are already changing the names of their teams and mascots.

  What do you think? How would you explain your point of view to a member of Washington's professional football team? To a Native American?

  How do you feel about other team names and nicknames, including the Vikings? Saints? Fighting Irish? Yankees?

Who decides what's acceptable and what's not? Who should decide? In the United States, the First Amendment to the Bill of Rights guarantees the "freedom of speech." Meanwhile, the concepts of "majority rule" and "let the people choose" are fundamental to the American system of government.

If some people decide that *Huckleberry Finn* is obscene, should all people be forbidden to read it? Should it be removed from public schools and libraries? At what point should "most people" say, "Wait a minute—this has gone too far"?

These questions don't have easy answers. What's important is to keep asking them as cultural attitudes continue to shift and change.

URBAN LEGENDS

You may find it troubling to learn that historical facts and cultural identity are more like gelatin than rock. Instead of being firm and solid, they wiggle and change, depending on the cultural climate.

But there is a positive side, too. The fact that history is continually being made, and culture is always being updated, means that *you* have a chance to make your mark on history and culture.

New myths are being born every day. Many are passed from friend to friend as true stories. They are made "real" by people like you. They are usually described as "something my friend saw" or "heard on the news" or "read in the paper." Most have an amazing aspect, but they are told seriously, as if they are the truth.

These modern-day urban legends are subjects of serious study. Scholars try to trace their origins, understand how they spread, and figure out what they say about our culture. You have probably heard several of these stories, such as the one about the cat in the microwave oven. Or the "Kentucky-fried rat" served at a local restaurant.

Often, urban legends contain gruesome or frightening details. A young man is driving home in the rain when he picks up a young woman who has missed her bus. It is late at night. The young man nearly runs into another car. When he catches his breath from the near-accident, he notices that the young woman is no longer in the car. She has left her book on the seat, with her name written inside. The next day, the young man tries to return her book. He finds her house, knocks on the door, and speaks to her father, who tells him that the young woman was killed in a car accident exactly one year ago.

Another urban legend was popular when girls used to wear beehive hairdos—helmet-like hair that was back-combed and

THERE ARE NO
CATS IN AMERICA

heavily sprayed. A girl refused to comb out her hair and wash it. Instead, she kept adding more hair spray to it. One day a black widow spider crawled into her hair, built a nest, and bit the girl, who died.

This may be more of a moral story than a myth, with the moral being, "If you don't wash your hair and go easy on the hair spray, something terrible will happen to you!" Does this remind you of anything? How about, "Cross your eyes and they'll stay that way"?

Some stories become a permanent part of a culture; others disappear almost instantly. It depends on what society views as important at the time. Conditions have to be just right for a story to be re-told enough to become an urban legend.

Myths are as ancient as ancient Greece and as current as tomorrow's gossip. They are a part of every culture. They may not be "true," but they are definitely real and valid. They are signs that a culture is vibrant and healthy. When myths become stale and can no longer move people emotionally, this indicates that a culture is dying. First the myths are lost, then the symbols, and finally the values based on the symbols. Dead cultures tell no tales.

COLLECTING URBAN LEGENDS

Many scholars study urban legends. You can join them or help out by collecting the ones you hear.

1. Arrange a situation where people are likely to share the urban legends they have heard. The less formal, the better. (Suggestions: a campfire, a slumber party.) If possible, videotape the event so you can record the storytellers' gestures and facial expressions, and the reactions of their listeners.

2. Write each story you hear in a special notebook. Date each entry and include what part of the country you heard it in (your home town? while on vacation in another state?). Note any observations you have about the story and the storyteller.

3. For each urban legend you collect, try to include the following information:

   a. the storyteller's name, age, and gender

   b. where the storyteller grew up

   c. where the storyteller got the story (who told it? when? in what part of the country?)

   d. whether the storyteller believes the story

e. what the storyteller thinks the story means

f. why the story was memorable to him or her.

4. Trace the story back as far as you can.

Where can you look for urban legends? You might investigate the myths surrounding your school. Or collect stories from your community. Compare and classify them. This might be a good group or class project—and fun besides.

People who study folklore are interested in your collection. You can send copies of your urban legends to:

Professor Jan Harold Brunvand
Department of English
University of Utah
Salt Lake City, UT 84112

Or there may be an American Folklorist at a college or university near you.

PERSONAL MYTHS

Imagine that you have just finished writing the story of your life as honestly as you could. Now imagine that your entire life up to now has been videotaped.

The two accounts would be very different. Your written autobiography would omit some details and exaggerate others. Events would run together. Your knowledge of things that happened after certain events would color your interpretation of those events. For example, if you were late to the airport and missed your flight, this would mean one thing at the time. If it later turned out that the flight you missed crashed, you would view the entire episode in a completely different light.

Like history and culture, your personal past tends to become more of a story than a strict relating of the five W's—who, what, when, where, and why. As events are retold, tales become taller, blues become bluer, and heroes and heroines become more heroic. Just as an actor on stage uses a loud voice and sweeping gestures to be heard and seen as "normal," you exaggerate your past to bring its full emotional meaning into the present, and to preserve the passion that was part of the original experience. You create your own autobiographical mythology. It becomes true for you.

"Television shows and commercials already teach us how to dress, wear our hair, talk to each other, and spend our leisure time. The home-video revolution induces us to think of our lives even more intensely in terms of T.V. The better our experiences fit on that screen in the living room for our friends and neighbors to see, the more 'real' they must be."

—Walter J. Gottlieb, television producer

THERE ARE NO CATS IN AMERICA

Cultural myths give individuals a way to relate as a group. Your personal myths give you a way to understand your life as a continuous process rather than a series of isolated moments. As you move through your life, you develop a sense of who you are, where you have come from, and where you are going. Your personal myths tie everything together.

TRUTH #6:
NOTHING IS AS EASY OR AS HARD AS IT LOOKS. NOTHING IS AS GOOD OR BAD AS IT SEEMS.

"Our life is an apprenticeship to the truth, that around every circle another can be drawn; that there is no end in nature, but every end is a beginning; that there is always another dawn risen on mid-noon, and under every deep a lower deep opens."

–Ralph Waldo Emerson

Part of your personal mythology is based on what you have learned about your family history. That history is passed down to you by those who experienced it, and by those who have heard it and re-told it over the years. The result is a lovely myth about your ancestry, much more real to you than a catalog of factual events could ever be.

The word "myth" doesn't always mean that a story is made-up or untrue. It can also mean that facts have been connected, rearranged, and interpreted to create a story. Logically, the story will vary slightly with each re-telling. Magically, each re-telling will contain a small part of the person doing the telling.

For instance, if your great-grandfather bought a horse that later won the Kentucky Derby, that in itself is a terrific story. But if your grandfather tells it to you, adding a detail about how his father (your great-grandfather) had to sell off part of his farm to buy the horse, the story becomes even better. And if your father puts in his two cents—about how his father (your grandfather) trained the horse—you end up with an exciting story that spans the generations and feels very real to you.

Maybe your great-grandfather only had to sell a few of his favorite horses to get the Derby winner. Still, it *felt* at the time as if the family were sacrificing much more. Maybe your grandfather only spent a short time with the horse. Still, it *felt* to him, as a small boy, that he was doing most of the training.

You can see how a family story develops a life of its own, taking on parts of the people who pass it along. These may not be the straight, plain facts, but they seem more true to you than anything in the world.

FIVE FAMILY MYTHS

In 1990, thousands of students in Oregon and Washington State took part in a Family History writing contest. Following are excerpts from some of their essays. Can you find the details that re-tellers have added over the years?

For example, see Becky Blanchard's story. Is it likely that her grandfather would have described the ship as "a tiny toy on a giant waterbed"? Or do you think Becky used this "update" to artistically enrich her story?

1. *Andrea Groener, fourth grade, Bear Creek School, Bend, Oregon.*

   "My great-great-granddad, Ole Nelson, lived in Wisconsin with his wife and six children. He worked in a fruit warehouse and didn't always make ends meet. In his spare time he fished for extra money.

   "His wife pleaded with him not to go, because she knew Lake Superior could be as dangerous as the ocean where storms could blow in without warning.

   "When he reached Lake Superior, clouds were slowly rolling in, but nobody seemed to notice. They fished happily. That is, until thunder and lightning started cracking. Huge waves started pounding until the boat capsized. My great-great-grandfather lost his life that stormy day.

   "His last words to his wife were, 'This will be my last fishing trip.'"

2. *Becky Blanchard, fifth grade, Adams Elementary, McMinnville, Oregon.*

   "The Liberty, an average-sized Navy ship, destined for the United States, was being boarded by 1,000 American servicemen. One of the servicemen, Harold Blanchard, was my grandfather. Also along for the trip to the United States was my grandfather's new wife and stepson.

   "The ship left the dock and began the voyage to America.

   "The trip to the U.S. was hard, and it seemed so long to my father! Day after day on a wide blue sea! Waves tossing the vessels as if playing a game of catch. Seagulls crying to the boat, asking it to play, as they flew through a boundless sky. When the stars came out the ship became a tiny toy on a giant waterbed.

   "As the sun rose high in the sky, chaos arose on the dock. They were there! The servicemen shouted and cheered

as they ran off the dock into the waiting arms of a family member, but my father hung back. He and my grandmother had come to a land they never knew, yet now called 'home.' They looked back into the waves. Somewhere beyond distant seas was a life they had left behind. But, with my grandfather, they began a new life, and they started by taking the first step off the boat onto the shores of the land of liberty, America."

3. Marcus Koch, ninth grade, Glendale High School, Glendale, Oregon.

"On rainy days when it is too wet to go outside, I would sit by the fire and listen to my grandmother tell stories about her days in Brooklyn and her trip to come out West. My favorite stories are about my grandfather whom everyone called Koch.

"As well as being a real-life hobo and miner, he was also an outlaw in Canada."

4. Kristin Jacobsen, Astoria High, Astoria, Oregon.

"The Jakobsen family lived in a small farming village in Hornsyld, Vejle, Denmark. When Anne and Jens' children were between the ages of 4 and 12, a severe depression hit Denmark. To complicate matters, Jens contracted a fatal case of tuberculosis. To make ends meet, Anne arranged for her sons, Jakob and Soren, to work for another family while she and her daughters were housekeepers for a different family.

"But the sons' jobs couldn't last forever. They were then faced with the decision of working day labor in Denmark or immigrating to America in hopes of finding better work and living conditions."

5. Nikki Sontag, sixth grade, Springbrook Middle School, Newberg, Oregon.

"Many people dream of finding a rich relative—I found mine! When William O'Brien died in 1878, his worth was estimated at over $12 million. My great-great-great-grand-uncle William O'Brien was a very rich man but unfortunately none of the money has reached me! However, I have been left with an exciting family history.

"After sailing from Ireland to New York as a child, William was lured to California by the Gold Rush of 1849. Wealth did not change William O'Brien much. He was a friendly and considerate man, loyal to his family and friends. He did not flaunt his money, but bought a large three-story house which he shared with his widowed sister and her three children. Known through San Francisco as the 'Jolly Millionaire,' William O'Brien died in 1878 leaving an estate worth millions.

"The money made by my great-great-great-grand-uncle is gone, but he left a rich history for me to explore and enjoy."

YOUR FAMILY MYTHS AND MEMORIES

- Do you have any family myths? Write them down the way you remember them being told to you. Then carefully check to see what little touches of your own you have added to the story. What do they reveal about how the story affected you?

- Write a story about a family event you remember—one that took place during your lifetime. Choose a story that's worth being passed on as a family legend.

- Find out how your own autobiographical memory works. Keep a journal or log of events in your life. After a few months have passed, write down the way you remember a particular event from a few months ago. Then compare your recollections with the journal entry you recorded at the time. Do your recollections seem more "true" than your journal entry? Has anything happened to give that event special meaning?

LIVING HISTORY

Did Abraham Lincoln love to read? Probably. Did he love to read at night, by the flickering light of the fireplace, or did he read by the soft glow of a single candle? Who knows? But details like these certainly make the story more colorful.

Sometimes the truth we hear about or read is not the way it happened. The simple, factual statement—"Abraham Lincoln loved to read"—does not convey the passion young Abe had for learning. Often, historical events become larger-than-life stories which grow larger with each retelling. Some details are omitted; others are exaggerated. The stories stop being totally true, but they are more realistic and interesting than "just the facts."

As you have seen, this happens with personal memories of your own childhood. It happens with your family history as it is passed down to you, and with national and world history as it is reported in books and textbooks. While this "selective memory" distorts the facts, it allows the symbolic and emotional meaning to come to the surface. This meaning may seem more real than what actually "happened." It connects us to the past more strongly than the facts alone.

> **"The truth is What Is; the truth is Reality. Anchored to that, a person may find all else manageable."**
>
> —Piers Anthony

Culture is an agreement among a large group of people to accept a certain set of attitudes, historical facts, and values as the truth. But what is perceived as true today can later be seen as false. What is right or acceptable now may someday be unacceptable and in poor taste.

Does this mean that there are no real values, no permanent historical facts, no fixed attitudes? Is it all a lie? Or does it mean that values, history, and attitudes are actually alive, and therefore changing? If you had your choice between "just the facts" and the facts peppered with feelings and opinions, which would you choose?

CHAPTER 7

ADVER-LIES

Paul Bunyan was the mightiest of loggers. It has even been said that he invented logging. He was taller than the trees in the forest, and he combed his beard with a fir tree. He roamed the forests from Maine to California with his big blue ox, Babe. His footprints were so large that they formed Minnesota's 10,000 lakes when they filled with water. His voice was so powerful that whole forests blew over when he shouted to his men. He logged the entire state of North Dakota in one week, then dug out Puget Sound. He invented a cross-country saw that mowed entire forests in a single day.

Was Paul Bunyan...
a. a myth?
b. a legend?
c. propaganda studied by the Russians?
d. an advertising gimmick?
e. an environmentalist's nightmare?
f. all of the above?

THE BIG TRUTH ABOUT PAUL BUNYAN

It's hard enough to tell truth from fiction. But when marketing, entertainment, politics, and legends all get thrown together, you *really* have a puzzle to solve! Some people call this advertising. A truer name might be "adver-lies."

You can't just dismiss it as one big lie. Nor can you accept it as the truth. What you have to do is learn the special language and not-so-secret methods which are used to get you to think in a certain way, choose a certain product, or vote for a certain candidate.

Take a deep breath, because you're about to enter a maze where nothing is what it seems to be.

No...that would be too easy. Some things *are* what they seem to be. The trick is to figure out which ones.

Take Paul Bunyan. On the surface, he appears to be a colossal nature-destroyer who wipes out whole ecosystems with a single breath. Can you imagine a lumber company creating such a character as its symbol? In the 1990's, this would be a poor choice. But it worked in the 1920's. The times were different; the thinking was different. The nation was growing, building—and destroying—with great enthusiasm.

Paul Bunyan was born when Archie Walker, an executive of the Red River Lumber Company in the upper Midwestern United States, decided that a giant lumberjack might help convince his customers on the west coast that Red River could fill any order, no matter how large. Walker's second cousin, W.L. Laughead, drew the Paul Bunyan character, basing it on two of the biggest workmen in the lumber yard.

Laughead also worked with Walker to write the Paul Bunyan stories. Babe, the big blue ox, was Laughead's idea.

Red River's first advertising booklet starring Paul Bunyan was 32 pages long. Copies were sent to lumber customers all over the country. At first, it wasn't successful, because the city people didn't understand the lumber language used in the stories. But when it did catch on, it did so in a big way.

Companies all over the world started stealing the stories. That was okay with the Red River Lumber Company; they *wanted* the stories to be copied. They loved the publicity. They didn't even copyright the stories, which were plagiarized everywhere. Even the Kremlin in Russia asked for copies. They planned to study them to learn American propaganda techniques.

Some people believed that Paul Bunyan was an actual person and wrote him letters. But the ultimate victory for Walker and Laughead came when *real* lumberjacks retold the stories for scholars, who recorded them at their colleges as "authentic folklore." In a 1933 version of the tales, a publisher's note says, "Like Robin Hood, Paul Bunyan is a legendary figure, sprung into being from stories told and retold by successive generations."

By now you have probably guessed that the answer to the Paul Bunyan question on page 103 is "all of the above." Had the character been created today, he might also have been...

g. a movie

h. a TV series

i. a Saturday-morning cartoon

j. a breakfast cereal

k. a bubble bath

l. a trading card

m. an action figure

n. a stuffed doll

o. and much more.

If Walker and Laughead were around today, they could probably make more money licensing Paul Bunyan products than selling lumber.

SELLING IDEAS AND IMAGES

Ever since Paul Bunyan's time, advertisers have worked to discover better and better ways to sell you not only products, but *ideas*. They have become so skilled at this that many advertisers today sell ideas instead of products.

You may think you're buying popularity, but you're only buying a pair of jeans. You may believe you're buying self-esteem or glamour, but you're simply buying shampoo.

When marketers interviewed people in the 1950's to discover which products they preferred and why, they learned something important. People didn't actually buy the products they said they preferred. Instead, their choices reflected what they thought made them look good to the interviewers.

For example, when people heard the question, "Do you prefer a Corvette or a sedan?", they would hear the "hidden" question, "Are you a person of style or an old fogy?" The people would answer "Corvette" in order to appear stylish. But when the time came to buy cars, they would go out and buy sedans.

Really listen to what commercials promise you'll get from the products they promote. They're selling ideas and images. You'll hear words like "confidence" and "respect" at least as often as words that tell you what a product is and does.

Have you ever heard an ad for jeans that says, "These will keep you warm and dry"? If you buy shampoo just to clean your hair, you can buy the least expensive brand, because all shampoos clean your hair about the same.

"You can fool all of the people all of the time if the advertising is right and the budget is big enough."

— Joseph Levine

"Advertising may be described as the science of arresting the human intelligence long enough to get money from it."

—Stephen Leacock

Deep down inside, most of us know that the whole purpose of advertising is to manipulate us. Yet we keep buying products in the hope that they will make us popular, powerful, respected, sophisticated, and happy.

WHOSE TARGET ARE YOU?

To your family and friends, you may be a warm and wonderful human being. But to advertisers, you're a statistic.

You fit into a particular group. The people in your group are "targeted" as buyers of specific types of products. This means that the products are designed to get the attention of someone just like you...someone of your age, at your economic level, with your needs and interests.

Advertisers want to make sure that their expensive TV ads reach the right "targets." They don't want to waste their messages on people who probably won't buy their products.

See for yourself. Watch four different types of programs on TV:

1. a soap opera,

2. a news program,

3. a cartoon, and

4. a sporting event.

While you watch, make a list of each program's advertisers. What does this tell you about the target audience?

Which programs are the following products most likely to be advertised on? What does this tell you about their targets?

- toys
- cereal
- candy
- amusement parks
- video games

- beer
- shaving cream
- laundry soap
- window cleaner

P.S. Maybe beer commercials are showing up on cartoon shows, too. A study by the Center for Science in the Public Interest reported that American children ages 8-12 could name more brands of beer than they could name U.S. Presidents.

TRICKS AND TRIGGERS

In the 1950's, marketers began doing in-depth interviews to discover what makes consumers tick. They found out that people act and react to certain carefully selected images.

For example, people will buy "beauty" more willingly than "soap," "health" instead of "oranges," and "prestige" instead of "cars." Marketers realized that they could use people's weaknesses to sell products, if they positioned their products as "cures" for people's emotional problems and needs.

Then marketers started researching colors and package designs to learn what would attract buyers. One experiment offered the same detergent in three boxes. The first box was mostly yellow, the second box was mostly blue, and the third was blue with splashes of yellow. People who used the detergents reported that the detergent in the yellow box was "too strong," the detergent in the blue box was "too weak," and the detergent in the blue and yellow box was "wonderful."

In another experiment, a store offered two of the same product for 29 cents instead of the normal price of 14 cents each. Sales went up.

The more the new marketing techniques were used, the more people wanted to buy, buy, buy! The next thing researchers learned was how to trigger responses—ways to make consumers slap their money down on the counter instead of thinking about their purchases.

For instance, the word "because" triggers an "agreement response." Ellen J. Langer, a social psychologist at Harvard, approached people waiting in line to use a copy machine. "Excuse me," she said, "I have five pages. May I use the Xerox machine because I'm in a rush?" Ninety-four percent of the people she asked let her move ahead of them in line. But when she said "Excuse me, I have five pages. May I use the Xerox machine?" only 60 percent let her go ahead in line.

Then Langer tried saying "Excuse me, I have five pages. May I use the Xerox machine because I have to make some copies?" Read the previous sentence again. Did she give a legitimate reason for wanting to go ahead in line? No. She just stuck the word "because" in the sentence. Yet this worked just as well as "I'm in a rush"—a genuine reason. The magic word was "because."

Want attention? Questions work. So do short sentences. Ed McMahon knows.* Politicians know. Now you know, too. Or would you be more likely to pay attention to a longer, more complete

"You. A millionaire. Ten times over. Just weeks from now. Sound good?"

—Pitchman Ed McMahon, Publishers Clearinghouse Sweepstakes TV ad

"Ambitious aims? Of course. Easy to do? Far from it."

—President George Bush

---

* Ed McMahon. Former sidekick for Johnny Carson on TV's *Tonight* show. Host of *Star Search*. Also spokesman for Publisher's Clearinghouse sweepstakes. Sells magazines. Comes in the mail. Big envelope. Stickers inside. Ask your parents.

statement like this one, describing language patterns used by advertisers and politicians to get your money or your vote?

Questions force you to pay attention because you're conditioned to respond. (Right? What do you think? Do you agree? Why do you agree?) Short sentences work because they are frequently used when someone is giving you vital information ("Fire!" "Look out!" "Help!" "Get out!")

Like words, situations can be triggers. For example, if you're choosing between two similar products and you don't know the actual value of the item, a higher price tag will trigger the idea of "quality" in your mind. Because you were probably raised to believe that you get what you pay for, you may be more likely to buy something if the price is raised than if the price is lowered.

Smart salespeople know that when you're presented with two choices, you'll compare them, and the comparison will automatically trigger certain responses in you. For instance, if you're shopping for gloves and a new coat, a savvy clerk will know to sell you the coat first, because even a very expensive pair of gloves will seem less expensive by comparison.

If you're shopping for a house, realtors may show you very run-down houses first. Then, when they take you to the house they want you to buy, it will look that much more terrific.

Of course, all of these triggers will be useless on you now. Or will they? Do you think it's fair to use these methods? Where do they fall on the Lie Line? (See "Where Do You Weigh In?" on pages 5-6.)

A MATTER OF STYLE

Did you ever wonder why there aren't more interesting programs on television? Maybe it's because researchers have learned that when TV shows are *too* exciting, the products advertised in the commercials don't sell as well. Viewers become more interested in the programs than the ads.

When a program is *too* funny, product messages don't get through. People tend to talk about the program during the commercials.

Another trick marketers use is to promote a certain style. Once everyone becomes aware of a skirt length, necktie width, sofa color, or car headlight shape, the marketers switch to a different style. People start believing that they need to buy new clothes, furniture, or cars so theirs won't look "out of date."

Marketers also create "personalities" for products. People "fall in love" with the products and develop "brand loyalty." Realizing that customers can be preconditioned to buy,

"I do not read advertisements— I would spend all my time wanting things."

—The Archbishop of Canterbury

marketers work to etch product stories on their minds. Camay soap is "glamorous"—and so, by extension, is the Camay user. Ivory soap (and the Ivory user) is "99 and 44/100 pure." A bran cereal/eater is "sensible" while the Lucky Charms cereal/eater is "fun." Munching on oatmeal is simply "the right thing to do."

Another effective technique is the loud, obnoxious, or even disgusting message. It doesn't matter if a commercial annoys you; what counts is whether the product name sticks in your memory. The "live egg-carrying roaches" featured in one commercial for bug spray left an unforgettable if repulsive image with the television viewer. The hearing-aid commercial which lowers the volume (so you think you need to get your hearing tested) is irritating, but it works. You don't forget it.

ADBUSTERS

Are you tired of TV and magazine ads full of stereotypes, sexism, and propaganda? So are a lot of other people. Read what they're doing about it in *Adbusters*, a quarterly magazine published in Vancouver, Canada. You'll learn about boycotts and tips on getting homemade, alternative ads on the air.

Ask your library to subscribe, or write to: Adbusters, The Media Foundation, 1243 West 7th Avenue, Vancouver, British Columbia V6H 1B7, Canada.

BETTER AND BEST

It's perfectly legal for advertisers to exaggerate what their product can do, as long as their claim can't be scientifically tested. In other words, it's okay for a company to say that its product gives you a "perfect complexion" or represents "the ultimate in freedom." This technique is called "puffing," and you can't take it to court.

It's also perfectly legal for advertisers to claim that their product is "the best," even though they can't claim it's "better" unless they have test results to prove it.

Follow this line of reasoning closely, if you can. Products which are made in basically the same way with basically the

> "Let advertisers spend the same amount of money improving their product that they do on advertising and they wouldn't have to advertise it."
>
> —Will Rogers

same ingredients are called "parity products." Parity products are considered to be equally good and equally bad. Since all parity products are essentially "the same," all can be called "the best."

You've just encountered a stunning and creative example of advertising logic. But there's more.

The law lets advertisers claim that their brand is "the best," but they can't say it's "better" unless it is being compared to a product in a different parity group. For instance, it would be legal to say that Paul Bunyan Orange Juice is "the best" orange juice, and "better" than Babe the Blue Ox Vitamins. But it would *not* be legal to say that Paul Bunyan Orange Juice is better than Pinocchio Orange Juice, since the two products are in the same parity group.

What does all of this twisted logic mean? In simple terms, it means that when a product is called "the best," it's really the same as all the other products in its group. Or, at least, there's no proof that the product is better than others which are supposed to do the same job. The word "best" is a tip-off to you that the product is a "parity" product. So when you see a product advertised as "the best," you may decide to choose a less expensive product in the same group.

It also means that since all people fall into the same category (homo sapiens), none can claim to be "better" than the others. But you can legitimately, legally say that you are THE BEST!

Remember: you read it here first, in the best book on lies ever written—better than any TV show or movie!

WEASEL WORDS

You now know the truth about "better" and "best," but there are other weasel words waiting to steal your money.

Weasels are animals that steal eggs from the nests of other animals. They make a small hole in the egg and suck out the insides. Then they place the hollow egg back in the nest, which appears to be undisturbed. Weasel words are named for this animal because they are empty and leave you with a false impression.

Here are some weasel words to watch for.

- **Virtually.** An ad claims that a product is "virtually trouble-free" or leaves clothes "virtually spotless." What is it really saying? Nothing! Think about how hollow the word "virtually" sounds. It means "being in essence or effect but not in fact." Do you want or need a product that is "not in fact trouble-free" or leaves clothes "not in fact spotless"?

- **Help.** A candy bar "helps." An aspirin "really helps." Beware of promises to "help"! This word is used to leave you with the impression that a product can solve a problem. But it leaves lots of room to wiggle out of a claim. How much will it help? What, exactly, will it help? How will it help? How long will it help?

- **Works Like Magic! Fast-Acting! Relieves Symptoms Fast with Regular Use!** "Works," "like," "magic," "fast," "acting" (or "acts"), "relieves," "regular use"—weasel words all. They don't say what you think they say. Think again.

What's the point of vague words and incomplete expressions? They leave blank spaces for you to fill in with images that fit you specifically. As you fill in the blanks, you feel as if the speaker understands you and is telling you the truth. You drift into a sort of daydream where the words seem to have been written just for you.

You're watching a commercial for a toilet-bowl cleaner. Suddenly the voice-over says, "It's like a walk in spring." The word "like" shifts your focus. You see yourself strolling along a beach or through the woods. You're left to fill in your own favorite image of spring. You forget all about toilet bowls. The next time you go shopping, you pick up a bottle of the product because, in the back of your mind, you remember that lovely walk in spring.

Still more weasel words to watch for:

- **Up To, Can Be.** That new gum lasts "up to five times longer." Five times longer than what? Your old brand of gum, or a chunk of rubber tire? That new cassette player "can be the most fun you'll ever have." But "can be" doesn't mean "will be."

- **Rich, Thick, Quick.** Creamy "rich," super "thick," extra "quick"—compared to what?

- **Scientifically Formulated.** Sound impressive? That's the point. But unless that deodorant is mixed up in a bucket in somebody's garage, and unless that hair conditioner is stirred up in somebody's kitchen sink, then of course it's "scientifically formulated." Everything is made according to a "formula," with certain measured-out amounts of certain ingredients. If you confuse the formula for anti-freeze with the formula for face powder, what you get is still "scientifically formulated."

And what about rhetorical questions? Wouldn't you really rather have an answer?

Naturally you're too smart to fall for the ads which use flattery. (If you fell for that one, you really *do* deserve to be fooled by advertisers!)

CAN YOU FIND THE WEASEL WORDS?

Read these slogans. How many weasel words can you find? Do you see any double meanings? Which ads want you to fill in your own images? What questions would you like to ask the companies behind the advertising?

1. "...prefer the taste two to 1 over the leading brand." (Tylenol Cold)

2. "Quantities are limited, so go to Sears today."

3. "Mazda. It just feels right."

4. "Oldsmobile. The look may change, but the spirit remains the same."

5. "Nothing carves the road like a Honda."

6. "Snickers satisfies the hunger inside you."

7. "When you're comfortable, you can really go places." (Cherokee shoes)

8. "Chiquita. Quite possibly the world's perfect food." (Chiquita Bananas)

9. "Introducing a whole new way to look at Pepsi and diet Pepsi."

10. "Now, more than ever." (A furniture store)

TOO GOOD TO BE TRUE

Advertisers sometimes make a game out of telling the truth without really telling the truth. It's like the child who goes to Mom and says, "If Dad says it's okay, can I go to the park?" Mom says, "Okay." Next, the child goes to Dad and says, "It's okay with Mom if I go to the park." Strictly speaking, the child isn't lying. But neither is the child telling the truth.

One commercial claims, "If it doesn't say Goodyear, it can't be polyglas." Why not? Because the Goodyear company has copyrighted the trade name "polyglas" for a fiberglass reinforcement. Any company can use the reinforcement in their products, but only Goodyear can call it "polyglas."

By now you can probably figure out for yourself what "doctors recommend" really means.

> "Advertising is the art of making whole lies out of half truths."
>
> —Edgar A. Shoaff

> ## TRUTH #7:
> ## YOU CAN'T GET SOMETHING FOR NOTHING. (OR: IF SOMETHING SEEMS TOO GOOD TO BE TRUE, IT PROBABLY IS.)

There are restrictions on how long the word "new" can be used to describe a product. But never fear, there are ways around this, too. Advertisers are clever wordmasters who seem to enjoy the challenge.

What do they use instead of "new"? How about "introducing," "now there's," "presenting," and "today's"—all clearly meant to give the impression of a "new" product. And a product can be called "improved" if it is changed even slightly. It doesn't have to be changed for the better, just changed.

LABEL LANGUAGE

Ad campaigns have made you more aware of labels and brands than your grandparents probably were at your age. How much do labels influence your actions and thinking? Do you apply them to people with certain views ("racist," "liberal," "skinhead"), social status and professions ("yuppie," "blue-collar," "white-collar"), and interests ("nerd," "jock")? Do you know any people who believe that it's important to wear a particular brand of clothes or shoes? How many labels could be pinned on you?

Labels for people aren't regulated by law, although some people think they should be. But labels for products must meet certain "truth in labeling" laws. These laws are designed to prevent product claims from becoming too deceptive. The U.S. government has cracked down on labels such as "lite," "cholesterol-free," and "high-fiber" that imply health benefits.

Sometimes a lie on a label is much more attractive than the alternative. Consider the case of the horrible "soup thing." It's enough to make the Jolly Green Giant turn white and the Campbell kids turn green.

According to a 1986 article in *The Wall Street Journal*, some food technologists got together and made up some "trash soups" for an unnamed company, "just for fun." The soups were made of ingredients which usually got thrown away—

minced cod, scallop mantels (the greenish, rubbery protective lips found in scallop shells), and the effluent (waste liquid) from a clam-processing plant. This effluent had formerly been dumped as sewage after it was used to clean the clams.

The "just-for-fun" soups were not called "trash soups." They were called "New England Clam Chowder" and "Manhattan Clam Chowder." They were a big hit. Soon after, the company started bottling the clam-cleaning water and selling it as "clam juice" for eight dollars a bottle.

BIGGER AND BETTER, OR SMALLER AND WORSE?

Check the food packages on your family's shelves. How many of these phrases can you find?

- "At least..."

- "As much as..."

- "Not more than..."

- "Less than..."

What do they really mean? What do the advertisers hope you will think they mean?

Now look at the weights listed on food cans and boxes. Only a few years ago, the standard-size can of tuna was 7 ounces. Today it might be 6 1/2 ounces, or even 6 1/8 ounces. What used to be a 16-ounce can of vegetables may now be only 14 1/2 ounces. The 1-pound box of cookies you bought last year might be just 14 ounces today.

The weights go down, but the prices go up. New York Attorney General Robert Abrams is asking for a law that would require downsized products to be labeled "reduced," "decreased," or "less" for at least six months after a change is made.

Now *that* would be truth in labeling.

Maybe you don't always want to know the truth behind the labels. Since many ingredients are given scientific labels, you are spared the gory details.

There are also legal restrictions on labeling something "budget size," "value pack," or "money-saving." For these terms to be used on a product label, there must be at least a five percent savings per unit weight over the original price. For example, if an 8 ounce bag of potato chips costs $1.60, or 20 cents per ounce, then the value pack must save you at least 1 cent an ounce—5 percent of 20 cents. A price of $3.04 for 16 ounces would fit the bill.

Label restrictions don't apply to food items only. Advertisements for new theater productions must state whether the production is still in previews. During previews, major changes are still being made in the cast, music, and text. Producers who don't label preview performances can be fined as much as $500.

"GREEN" ADVERTISING

Marketers keep finding new ways to mislead and lie to consumers. And consumers keep asking for new laws to keep them informed about what they are really buying. Often, the laws lag behind.

In recent years, marketers have hit on a very successful way to translate buyers' good intentions into dollars for themselves. By cashing in on shoppers who are concerned about the environment, companies are turning the "green" of environmentalism into the "green" of money.

In 1990, sales of so-called "green" products came to nearly two billion dollars. They are expected to increase to nine billion dollars in the not-too-distant future. The fact that there's so much money involved is your clue to keep your eyes and ears open.

Some wary consumers have realized that terms like "safe for the environment" and "environment-friendly" are too vague to be meaningful. Not all "good-for-the-Earth" labels are telling the truth. Products "made with recycled paper" can use only a small percentage of recycled paper and still make the claim. "Biodegradable" containers don't break down when they are buried in landfills, which is still where most trash ends up.

People who are genuinely concerned with the environment are demanding standardized definitions for these and other terms. They want to make sure that truly "green" products are the only ones raking in the green dollars. They don't want to hear half-truths and adver-lies.

"You can tell the ideals of a nation by its advertisements."

—Norman Douglas

Until advertisers are *completely* truthful about environmental claims, you'll do the environment more good by *not* buying questionable products.

THE POWER OF ADVERTISING

How have marketing techniques and technology changed people's behavior and thinking? Are we more concerned with appearances than our grandparents were? Do we see poor people as human beings or "image problems"? When children grow up with constant advertising, do they learn that they "need" certain products and labels to be accepted by their peers? Does advertising inform or confuse? Does it make us more honest or more phony?

These are questions to consider as you're hit with advertising on TV, radio, and in magazines. The more you think about advertising, the more questions you start to ask. The more questions you ask, the more answers you find. And the more answers you find, the better informed you become.

You may discover that advertising has its good points, too. For example, those big signs in your local ball park aren't there just for looks. Companies pay money to advertise in sports facilities. They know that many people will see their ads. Meanwhile, the money they pay helps to keep ticket prices lower than they would be without advertising revenues.

Before marketers discovered us as buyers/consumers, we thought of ourselves as workers/producers. There are basic differences in these two self-images.

- Workers/producers are inner-directed and create things out of their own energy and ideas. Buyers/consumers are outer-directed and use things up ("consume" them).

- Workers/producers pay attention to the price of a product. Buyers/consumers are persuaded by the packaging.

- Workers/producers choose leaders who are practical and honest and friends who like them for themselves. Buyers/consumers choose leaders and friends for their "image" and "personality."

- Workers/producers eat food. Buyers/consumers eat ingredients.

If you buy a product to make yourself feel beautiful, smart, powerful, or accepted, you may be using products in the same way some people use alcohol or other drugs: to create a "feeling."

If you hear people say that they voted for a candidate who "made them feel good about themselves," or that a policy of their country "made them proud," pause to think about it. Don't these sound like the same weasel words used in advertising? ("Gargle Mouthwash makes you feel good about yourself all day....Stay Cool Deodorant makes you proud to be a teen....") The buyer/consumer mentality leaves us open to empty promises, meaningless statements, and fake feelings.

Marketers have spent years and many, many dollars researching consumer attitudes and behaviors. But all they have really done is to change your mind. You can change it back again. You can be a wise consumer, buying the things you really need without being duped by adver-lies.

Imagine that you're at the store, holding a product labeled "environmentally safe." You can buy it to "feel good about yourself." You can tell yourself that it's "someone else's job" to make sure the claim is true. Or you can think like a worker/producer and ask yourself, "Do I really need this? Could I borrow it from someone else, or go without it?"

If you take this same approach to choosing friends, you'll look for people who share your interests, not necessarily those who wear the most expensive clothes. You'll look beyond their packaging and labels to what's inside. You'll hear the difference between empty promises and sincere offers for help, between polite flattery and genuine encouragement.

For over 40 years, marketers have been learning about us as consumers. But we have learned a lot about marketers, too. We've found that what we see is not always what we get. We have learned to ask questions about products and product claims—"If it doesn't work, can I return it?" "Is it guaranteed?" "Does it come assembled?" "Are batteries included?"

Advertising hype has forced us to question what we hear, see, and read—not just about products, but about scientific studies and political campaigns. Adver-lies challenge us to make choices more carefully and to live more thoughtfully— to pay attention, or pay the price.

TEN TIPS TO KEEP FROM BEING RIPPED OFF

Caveat Emptor. "Let the buyer beware." That old Roman saying is still good advice, even if it is thousands of years old.

Advertisers aren't going to watch out for you. Here's how to watch out for yourself.

1. **Read everything—especially the small print.** You'll find out some fascinating facts. For example, Haagen Dazs ice cream may sound Scandinavian, but it's really made in Teaneck, New Jersey. Copycat Frusen Gladje is made in Philadelphia, Pennsylvania.

2. **Don't sign anything which has blank spaces.** This includes contracts, checks, and agreements.

3. **Get everything in writing (and keep copies for yourself).** An oral agreement is only worth the paper it's written on.

4. **Beware of "bait-and-switch" ads.** It's illegal to advertise something at an incredibly low price just to attract customers, then "switch" them to another item when they come into the store. If this happens to you, report it to local authorities such as the Better Business Bureau.

5. **Know your rights.** You don't have to pay for anything that comes in the mail if you didn't order it, as long as you don't use it. Return it at the sender's expense. Read the guarantees that come with the products you buy.

6. **Be suspicious of "too-good-to-be-true" offers.** Your own greed can be your worst enemy. If something sounds too good to be true, it probably isn't true. If you send for "genuine diamonds" that are advertised at only $5 each, don't be surprised when they arrive—and look like grains of sand.

7. **Never give out personal information on the phone.** You may be conditioned to politely answer questions, but this habit is worth breaking when it comes to telling strangers about yourself. You don't know that callers are who they say they are. You don't know how they will use the information you give them. Simply say, "Sorry, I'm not interested," and hang up.

8. **Never pay any money for something you have "won" or something that's supposed to be "free."** Free means free. If you have to spend any of your money or time for something you have "won," then you haven't "won" anything.

   Beware of this common scam: Someone calls and says, "If you can answer a question, you'll win a prize!" The question is something absurdly simple. When you answer correctly, you're told that your prize will be delivered as soon as you send money "for postage and handling."

9. **Take your time.** Don't be pressured into buying something because it's your "last chance," "a limited offer," "one of a kind," or "a golden opportunity." Remember that there's *no* material item you literally "can't live without."

10. **Never forget that you can't get something for nothing.** This is the bottom line. Put it first on your personal list of buying do's and don'ts.

TAKE ACTION!

Do you babysit, or do you have younger brothers and sisters? Does reading this chapter make you want to take action? The American Psychological Association offers the following suggestions to help kids under age 7 who are sometimes unable to figure out all the adver-lies they see on cartoon shows.

- Be a translator for the kids in your life. Tell them that "partial assembly required" really means "you have to put it together."

- Tell them that the purpose of advertising is to sell, not to inform.

- Take them to a toy store to look at advertised toys. Point out the differences in the actual toy on the shelf and the "as advertised" toy. Did the radio-controlled car on TV look bigger, faster, brighter, and more fun than the one in the box?

- Teach them how to read ingredients lists on packages. Point out that the ingredient listed first is one the product contains the most of.

Spend time watching TV with a toddler or younger child. Point out some of the things you have learned in this chapter. Talk about weasel words and empty promises. Play a game to see who can spot the most weasel words during a half-hour program; to make it more fun, you might call it "Pop Goes the Weasel" and shout "POP!" whenever you spot a word.

CHAPTER 8

ALL HAT AND NO CATTLE

. . . .

You have until midnight tonight to get your picture on the front page of a national newspaper. If you don't succeed, you'll turn into a toad. Will you...
a. reveal that you have discovered a new planet?
b. beg newspapers to print your picture, explaining your toadish problem?
c. ride a graffiti-painted lion across the White House lawn?

. . . .

DO YOU HAVE A FUTURE IN PUBLIC RELATIONS?

If you answered "a" and were seriously thinking that this important story would get you a lot of attention, then you're probably not cut out for public relations work—or PR work, for short.

If you answered "b," you really have no idea how to get attention in the 20th century. Furthermore, you're trapped in a fantasy world if you honestly think that 1) anyone would believe your weird story, and 2) anyone would care if you did turn into a toad.

If you answered "c," then you may have a future in PR. Public relations people are hired by individuals, groups, or companies who need to make the front page by midnight...or else! The PR person's job is to keep them in the news; to make sure they are seen in all the right places, with all the right people; and to create a positive image. Riding a graffiti-painted lion across the White House lawn is all in a day's work. PR people *make* news.

BEHIND THE HEADLINES

The public relations stunt was invented by a man named Edward L. Bernays. In the 1920's, he caused a huge sensation by convincing wealthy New York women to light up "torches of freedom"—cigarettes—on Fifth Avenue. The purpose of the stunt was to combat the negative image people had of women smoking. Bernays knew that his idea would generate a lot of press coverage—free advertising for his client.

Public relations is about image, not fact. PR pros are concerned with how things "seem," not with how they are. And they think of everything.

For instance, they consider the impression that will be created by choosing a particular interviewer. If the interviewer won't make their client look good, then the interview won't be granted. A sensitive interviewer is chosen to make a weak political candidate look tough by comparison. A relaxed, down-to-earth interviewer makes an overly sophisticated candidate look relaxed and friendly.

PR people don't see themselves as distorting the truth, any more than special effects people do when they make it appear that a starship is traveling through space. Both kinds of professionals are simply "doing their job."

If you're ever called before a Congressional committee for questioning, bring your PR people along. They'll make sure that you're seated at a great big table so you appear small, picked-on, and sympathetic.

> **"Newsworthy events involving people usually do not happen by accident. They are planned deliberately to accomplish a purpose, to influence ideas and actions."**
>
> —Edward L. Bernays

HOW WOULD YOU DO IT?

A famous but unlikely person has decided to run for President and hired *you* to run his or her PR campaign. How will you make that person *seem* strong, smart, educated, and "presidential"? What will you have him or her say and wear? Who will he or she appear with, and where will they be seen? Come up with an unusual approach...maybe the truth. That would be different!

POLITICS AND PR

Have you noticed any similarities between advertising campaigns and political campaigns? Both use highly paid experts behind the scenes. If you have ever wondered why political announcements and speeches contain weasel words and symbols instead of solutions, now you know.

These professionals use every trick of persuasion they know, and they know a lot of them. Simple statements, repetition, emotional appeals, stirring music, graphic images, bold symbols, staged "spontaneous" events, and special effects are all part of the persuasive package. They have little to do with politics, but a lot to do with shaping voters' thoughts and opinions. PR people tell their candidates what to say, how to say it, and when to say it. They teach them to dodge the issues that really matter, in favor of "sound bites" that look good on the TV news.

In election year 1986, in the New Hampshire primary, Vice President Bush was running against Senator Robert Dole. The opponents of Senator Dole flipped his picture in TV ads so his hair was parted on the wrong side. Meanwhile, Vice President Bush's head was outlined by a thin halo of light.

Dole's words were framed in black or underlined in hot-tempered red. Bush's words were framed and underlined in calm blue. In scenes of the two candidates being greeted by crowds, Bush supporters were colorfully dressed and backed by cheers on a soundtrack, even though they appeared to be sitting quietly. Dole supporters were shown in washed-out colors.

Most so-called "spontaneous" political events are staged by professionals. During his acceptance speech at the 1980 Republican national convention, Ronald Reagan paused and said, "I have just thought of something that is not part of my speech, and I am worried about whether I should do it." He then made some dramatic remarks. In fact, the whole "spontaneous" episode was planned by Reagan's "handlers."

The people reporting the news gradually become part of the persuasion, whether they want to or not. No matter how honest a communicator tries to be, opinions sneak into his or her work. The same thing happens to you when you write an essay. You try to be fair and to present both sides equally, but you tend to select facts and views which support and agree with your own.

Even something as insignificant as a newscaster's smile may influence people. Shortly before the 1984 U.S. presidential election, social psychologist Brian Mullen and his colleagues performed an interesting experiment. They asked 45 college students to watch segments of network newscasts which contained references to the two candidates, Ronald Reagan and Walter Mondale. With the sound off, the students rated the facial expressions of the anchormen from extremely positive to extremely negative. The students rated Peter Jennings as having the most positive facial expression of all the anchors when referring to Reagan.

Six months after that election, Mullen and his colleagues telephoned 160 randomly selected people in four cities across the United States. They asked, "Who did you vote for?" and "Which network news anchorman did you watch most?" They found that the people who had voted for Reagan had most often watched Peter Jennings.

A match—or a coincidence? Were voters influenced by Jennings' smiling presentation when he spoke of Reagan? Or did they already prefer Reagan and tune into the newscaster who was most positive toward "their" candidate? Nobody knows for sure. But it seems possible that a newscaster's smile can influence the vote.

There will always be people who would like you to make decisions based on images rather than information. Usually, it's easier to scan an image than to seek out and weigh information, easier to accept than investigate. People tend to do what takes the least effort. The result is a partnership of ignorance.

When faced with a media image, always ask yourself two questions:

1. *What do I think about this?*

2. *What do the creators of the image want me to think, and why?*

DESPOTS, DICTATORS, AND OTHER MISLEADERS

Adolf Hitler used tricks of imagemaking and persuasion to try to accomplish his goal of taking over the world. He even tried to hire Edward Bernays to do his PR, but Bernays refused to work for Hitler. So Hitler studied American advertising and PR techniques on his own.

If you doubt the power of these techniques, read about Hitler and how far he got with his plan. A whole nation seemed to quit asking questions and thinking for themselves. They almost appeared to be...hypnotized.

One of Hitler's most effective and evil techniques was "the big lie." Ironically, he used the basic *goodness* of people to trick them into going along with his plot. The bigger the lie, he reasoned, the more likely the German people would accept it. Why? Because most average people tell little lies, but they are ashamed to tell big ones.

Hitler figured that the German people simply would not recognize a huge lie. They would be unable to believe that someone would do the things he was planning to do. "The vast masses of a nation are in the depths of their hearts more easily deceived than they are intentionally bad," he said.

Hitler knew that reason is the enemy of propaganda. So he made use of emotional, irrational appeals. He much preferred the ignorant mob to an educated group. He said, "Education for all is a disintegrating poison invented by Liberalism for its own destruction."

What if the German people had refused to listen to Hitler's message? What if they had insisted on hearing the facts? What if other people in other nations in the future *don't* insist on facts and meaningful messages?

"Once in every man and nation Comes the moment to decide, In the strife of Truth and Falsehood For the good or evil side."

—James Russell Lowell

DO YOU FALL FOR THESE PR TECHNIQUES?

During the 1600's, Pope Urban VIII organized a *congregatio de propaganda fide*—a "congregation for propagating the faith." The intent was to spread Christianity by locating missions throughout the world.

In spite of its original purpose, the word "propaganda" now carries with it the implication of influencing someone for evil

purposes. Here are a few propaganda techniques that are used to persuade you.

1. **Name-calling.** A simple technique of labeling a person or a group. Example: "witches," "liars," "welfare cheats."

2. **Generalities.** The act of throwing out undefined and unsupported statements. Examples: "gentlemen prefer blondes," "all teenagers are lazy." (Tip: Watch for statements that begin with "all" or "none.")

3. **Testimonials.** Recommendations from authorities, experts, and stars. "Four out of five doctors recommend...." "Bo knows...."

4. **"Plain folks."** Appeals to the "regular people." Example: "If you're like most folks, you long for simpler times...."

5. **Stacked deck.** Giving just one side of an argument. Example: Any political advertisement.

6. **Bandwagon.** Appeals to the masses. Examples: "Everyone is doing it!" "The polls show...."

PERSECUTION, SECRETS, AND MISLEADING LANGUAGE

Despots and dictators have always known how to get ahead: by blaming some group, race, or class of people for the troubles their country is having. They know that most people don't want to face their own failure to demand good leadership.

We have seen this happen again and again, all through human history. Hitler persecuted the Jews and the Gypsies; Saddam Hussein persecuted the Kurds.

If there is no group handy to accuse, one can always be created. This happened with the Salem, Massachusetts witch trials of 1692. In the 1950's, many Americans believed that "communists" were hiding everywhere, ready to take over the country.

Truly diabolical leaders may even create hardships intentionally, then step in and appear to save the day. They will do whatever it takes to win, from small-scale cheating to large-scale lying.

Even with good leaders and educated citizens, a government and its people may have a hard time agreeing about how much the citizens should be told, and how much truth they can bear to hear. Governments claim to keep secrets "for the good of the public." But since the public can't know the secrets, they can't tell if the government has a good reason to keep secrets from them. This may create a climate of distrust.

Government officials may even have their own political language. Kazuhisa Inoue, a member of the Japanese Parliament, has asked the Japanese government to try to change its misleading language. He has made a list of 51 expressions Japanese politicians use which ordinary Japanese citizens can't understand.

Inoue is also concerned with how this misleading language affects communication with foreign governments. For instance, when a Japanese Cabinet minister says, "We shall make efforts," it really means, "Nothing at all will be done." Other Japanese politicians understand this, but foreign governments don't. Similarly, "I will accomplish it with greatest expedition possible" means "I will go as slowly as possible." "Let me think about it" means "No."

WHAT DO YOU MEAN?

Is there someone you have trouble communicating with? Someone whose "maybe" means "no," whose "later" means "never," whose "okay" means "maybe," and so on? You don't have to go to the Japanese government to find this particular "foreign" language.

What do YOU mean when you say "yes," "no," "maybe," "okay," "soon," "later," "great," etc.? Are you communicating clearly? If not, how can you start saying what you mean, and meaning what you say?

DO WE REALLY WANT TO KNOW THE TRUTH?

On July 4, 1966, the United States Freedom of Information Act was signed into law. It gives any U.S. citizen the right to see any official document unless the government can prove that it falls into a "protected category." These categories include:

- military secrets,
- law enforcement secrets,
- sensitive financial or business data,
- privacy rights of individuals,
- some internal government documents, and
- some geological material.

With the signing of the act, Americans can finally know the truth! But do they really want to know it? And how much of it do they really want to know?

It's easy to conceal a truth when one side doesn't want to tell it and the other doesn't want to hear it. Plus this helps misleaders to keep misleading.

For example, both government and business leaders hate to tell the people when the economy is doing poorly, but not as much as the people hate to hear it. Business leaders may be afraid that informed people will start worrying about their jobs and stop buying things, which will make the economy worse. Government leaders may fear that people will blame them for the economy and won't reelect them.

In 1956, the U.S. economy was weak. Meanwhile, business leaders were talking loudly about their "optimism." They felt "confident of a rising economy." Everything they said was carefully planned to convince the public that things were going well. Here is the way *Tide*, a professional journal, reported the situation:

> "These men aren't talking just to hear their voices, nor do they enjoy venturing out on an economic limb. Their main aim is to beef up the confidence level of the nation by counteracting pessimism that sometimes get voiced, so that dealers will keep on ordering goods and consumers will keep on buying goods, at a higher and higher rate, and if necessary go into debt to do it. To maintain a pace of increasing consumption, a high level of credit buying must be maintained as well."

The economy always moves up and down through natural cycles; this is a proven historical fact. Still, people are shocked and dismayed at every downturn. They get scared.

They get so scared that these economic down times used to be called "panics." Then people started fearing that word, so they began calling panics "recessions." This made everyone feel better for a time.

When Herbert Hoover was President, the economy entered a panic...er, that is, a recession. But Hoover insisted on calling it "just a little depression." As it turned out, the "little depression" made the recessions of the past look like good times. Today we're back to using the word "recession" instead of "panic" or "depression." A popular joke goes, "A recession is when your neighbor loses his job. A depression is when you lose yours."

Maybe changing the words changed the way people responded to the truth. Maybe more decisive action might have been taken sooner, and led to a better outcome, if the "little depression" had been called a "panic."

While PR people are busy helping to create the news and manage people's impressions, journalists merely report the news—or is there more to their job than that? In fact, journalists can and often do create impressions by the way they report events. Sometimes this is intentional. Sometimes opinions sneak in by accident.

Compare how journalists Ms. Bo and Mr. Peep report the same events:

- In Ms. Bo's article, you read: "The banker *said* he was in Bermuda when the money disappeared."

- In Mr. Peep's article, you read: "The banker *claimed* he was in Bermuda when the money disappeared."

- Bo: "The reporter *observed* the three-legged cow in the farmer's barn."

- Peep: "The reporter *discovered* the three-legged cow in the farmer's barn."

- Bo: "The Senator *said* he was at the scene of the crime."

- Peep: "The Senator *admitted* he was at the scene of the crime."

How are their articles different? Which reporter's articles would you rather read, Bo's or Peep's? Whose writing seems less emotional and opinionated?

The meaning and impact of news stories can be changed by adding pictures or charts, or by giving them large or small headlines. Where a story is placed also influences how significant it seems. If it's on Page One, it must be important; if it's buried in the middle, it must be less important. Many newspapers place their business news within the sports section. What does this suggest to you?

Minor manipulations like these can lead to major impressions and misperceptions. But how often do most readers notice them? How often do you notice them?

"When a boy tells a lie it can cause trouble; but when a newspaper tells a lie it can cause more trouble. People are liable to find the newspaper a hundred years from now and believe it."

— Wyatt Earp

"You should always believe all you read in the newspapers, as this makes them more interesting."

—Dame Rose Macauley

CAN YOU TRUST YOUR SOURCES?

Thomas Jefferson believed that newspapers should be divided into four sections: "Truth, Probability, Possibility, and Lies."

He went on to say, "Advertisements contain the only truths to be relied on in a newspaper."

Yet he defended those same newspapers he had criticized with, "Were it left to me to decide whether we should have a government without newspapers or newspapers without government, I should not hesitate a moment to prefer the latter."

You're reading through a newspaper when you see these two headlines: "RUSSIANS BUY WITH ABANDON" and "U.S. ECONOMY SUFFERS ANOTHER DECLINE." What do you conclude about the economies of Russia and the United States just from reading these headlines? It might appear that the Russians have plenty of money, while the U.S. is going broke.

In fact, at the time these headlines appeared, the Russians were "buying with abandon" because they knew that prices were about to soar. Their economy was in much worse condition than that of the United States.

If you read only the headlines, you might get a false or inaccurate picture of the way things really are.

A newspaper is just one source of information. You can't have the truth if you limit yourself to one source, because you'll be getting the reporting (and opinions) of the same people all the time.

Not all sources are equally reliable when it comes to telling the truth. For instance, if you get your facts from the *Congressional Record,* you know they must be true, right? Actually, wrong. The U.S. Constitution gives Congress the right to lie. Members of Congress can't be held accountable for "any speech or debate in either House." And they "shall not be questioned in any other place." They can say anything—*anything*—in a speech or debate and insert it into the *Congressional Record.*

If you ever believed in Santa Claus, it was because you trusted the source of your information—your parents. You overlooked the facts that didn't fit. You may not have questioned the story as much or as soon as you might have if you had gotten it from a different source.

Another very real possibility is that the news is just plain wrong. Alfred Nobel, the inventor of dynamite, once read about his own death in the newspaper. The paper didn't say kind things about him or his invention. Shocked at how the paper portrayed him, Nobel decided that he wanted to be remembered in a more positive light, so he established the Nobel Peace Prize.

PROJECT CENSORED

Sometimes the media focus on one story and ignore others in order to shape your opinion. Many important stories go almost unnoticed.

Project Censored is a program of Sonoma State University in California. Each year, Project researchers collect stories from newspapers around the country. At the end of the year, they choose what they consider to be the "ten most censored stories" and publish a list describing them.

Project Censored defines censorship as "the suppression of information, whether purposeful or not, by any method—including bias, omission, or under-reporting—which prevents the public from fully knowing what is happening in its society."

These were some of the stories they listed for 1991:

- **The Gulf War.** During the war, reporters videotaped the devastating effects of the war on the Iraqi countryside and Iraqi civilians. Both CBS and NBC refused to air the footage.

- **The Savings and Loan scandal.** Government staffers were told to "play down" the Savings and Loan crisis during the 1988 presidential campaign so they wouldn't hurt George Bush's chances for the Presidency. Had they spoken up, they could have saved the country $250 billion, according to Federal Home Loan Bank Board officials.

- **The right to information.** The Freedom of Information Act gives citizens access to official government documents, unless the government can prove that they must be kept secret. During the Reagan and Bush administrations, the people's right to information has been sharply reduced.

- **Corporations and the environmental movement.** Corporations have been sabotaging the efforts of environmentalists and infiltrating environmental groups. These stories have not been reported in the mainstream media.

Is there a news story you think Project Censored should know about? Send a copy, including the source and the date, to:

Dr. Carl Jensen
Director
Project Censored
Sonoma State University
Rohnert Park, CA 94928

CHECKING YOUR SOURCES

You might think that dictionaries are totally truthful and completely objective, but think again.

- Noah Webster, creator of the first Webster's Dictionary, intentionally filled it with his moralistic opinions, hoping to influence the public.

- The Russian edition of the *Oxford Student's Dictionary of Current English* redefined "communism," "imperialism," "marxism," and "fascism" in favorable language. For example, it defined "socialism" as "a social and economic system which is replacing capitalism."

- Consider the objectivity of this entry from the *Morris Dictionary of Word and Phrase Origins:*

  beat/beatnik. Kerouac, we believe—had the consummate bad taste to invent an origin for the term. Beat, he opined, was short for "beatified," thus sanctifying himself and his talentless fellow travelers....With the passage of years the West Coast beats have either disappeared or become respectable.

Check your own favorite dictionary. How objective is it?

SMALL WORDS, BIG IMPRESSIONS

PR people and journalists aren't alone in using words to create impressions. Members of the legal profession do it, too. For instance, a judge in the courtroom says, "Please approach the bench," not "Come up here and talk to me." Using the third person ("the bench") places the judge on a higher, more authoritative level.

The job of the defense attorney in a trial is to make the crime seem as vague and unreal as possible. He or she tries to put distance between the accused person and the deed. Watch a real trial on TV, and you'll notice that the defense lawyer uses passive verbs and abstract language, while the prosecuting lawyer uses active verbs, concrete language, and as many facts as possible.

For instance, the defense might say, "After some unsuccessful attempts...," but the prosecution would say,

"They tried twice. They were unsuccessful." By using confusing language and vague words, the defense tries to get the jury to focus on generalities, not facts, and think less critically.

Even a small word change can create a new impression. In one experiment, people were shown a film. Afterward, they were asked one of two questions: 1) "Did you see *the* broken headlight?" or 2) "Did you see *a* broken headlight?" When the word "the" was used in the question, twice as many people said that they had seen a broken headlight—even though none appeared in the film.

> "I prefer the word 'homemaker' because 'housewife' always implies that there may be a wife someplace else."
>
> —Bella Abzug

HOW TO NEVER TELL A LIE

If you choose, you can never tell a lie again. Instead, simply "utter a falsehood," "buy into a myth," "make an inoperative statement," "speak out of turn," "misspeak," or "utter an inconsistency."

All of these are euphemisms for the word "lie." They are ways to say "lie" without actually using the word.

Substitute words are often used for unpleasant subjects we don't want to talk about. Have you ever heard someone speak of "losing their loved one" or having the loved one "pass away"? We all know what happened to that loved one, but nobody says the dreaded D-word.

Substitute words can't change the truth, but they can cover it up and influence your actions and feelings. Would you rather be a gardener or a landscaper? A waitress or a hostess? Would you rather own an old house or a restored Victorian? You get the idea.

Below are some more pleasant-sounding words used for unpleasant truths. Can you guess what they really mean?

1. Collateral damage

2. Arbitrary deprivation of life

3. Negative patient outcome

4. Vintage clothing

5. Vertically challenged

6. Preowned car

7. Maintenance engineer

Find the answers on pages **157-158**.

EXPOSING EUPHEMISMS

The *Quarterly Review of Doublespeak* is a publication of the National Council of Teachers of English. Four times a year, this fascinating review exposes verbal cover-ups found in magazines, newspapers, speeches, and official announcements. Here are some examples from a recent issue.

- A stock analyst referred to "dedicated entertainment hardware"—video games.

- The computer files at an insurance company were "inadvertently cleared"—erased.

- An advertisement offered readers a "second once-in-a-lifetime opportunity."

- During the Gulf war, the Saudi government had a hard time dealing with the idea of female soldiers, who made up one-tenth of the U.S. forces. So the Saudis called them "males with female features."

- When a White House official took advantage of his position by using government transportation for personal reasons, another official announced, "He didn't do anything wrong and he'll never do it again."

- The U.S. Senate voted itself a "pay equalization concept"—a raise.

- According to the U.S. Department of Agriculture, cows, pigs, and sheep are "grain consuming animal units."

- A California newspaper refers to fat people as "calorically disadvantaged."

Are you hungry for more doublespeak? Ask your library to subscribe to the Quarterly Review, or write to:

Quarterly Review of Doublespeak
National Council of Teachers of English
1111 Kenyon Road
Urbana, IL 61801

PACING: A TRUST-GAINING TACTIC

Before other people can influence you, they must first gain your trust. If you trust, then you believe. If you believe, then you accept the ideas or opinions the people you trust are presenting to you. Gaining trust is the primary goal of all persuasive techniques.

One popular trust-gaining tactic is called "pacing." In its most basic form, pacing means reflecting someone else's movements, breathing rate, and manner of talking. The idea is to get the other person to think, "We are alike." After that, influencing the other person is easy. Ideas, suggestions, and opinions which actually come from outside of you seem to come from inside. It's almost as if you are a puppet, and the persuader is pulling your strings.

- "Descriptive pacing" uses simple, factual statements to enter another person's world and gain his or her trust. For example, you might say, "It has been cold this winter, hasn't it?" or "I see you have arrived at exactly 3:30." You're simply stating *what* is. The other person hears you telling the truth and starts to trust you. He or she is less likely to question later statements containing hidden commands, meanings, assumptions, or questions.

- "Objection pacing" uses shared disagreement to build trust. You start out by agreeing with the person you want to win over. You might nod your head, look sympathetic, and say things like, "I don't blame you. I'd be upset, too." Gradually, using persuasive language, you move him or her to your way of thinking.

- A third pacing technique uses "matching words." For example, if the other person says, "I hear you," you say, "Then listen to this." "Look at this" would not match.

A speech given by President Bush in 1990 was a masterpiece of pacing. Addressing an environmental conference, the President referred to "a climate of good will," "an atmosphere of controversy," and "the heat of politics." With the words "climate," "atmosphere," and "heat," he entered the internal emotional world of his environmentally aware audience. By creating a sense of trust, he discouraged the tendency to question.

Peggy Noonan is a brilliant speech writer who has worked for Presidents Reagan and Bush. She explains that speech writers fashion each word and phrase in a Presidential speech so it is most effective. Nothing is left to chance. For instance, she points out that a good speech writer would notice a sentence beginning with "frankly." That word would be removed from a speech because it suggests, "At other times, I am not being frank." It makes the speaker appear untrustworthy.

"And man slowly discovered the errors in his original world. He learned to distrust what things told him, and gradually he forgot the world of birds and stones. Instead he developed a new activity which he called thinking. Reason seemed to reveal truth, but a truth that would give no guidance to conduct."

—Kurt Koffka

TRICK QUESTION

Which would you prefer?

1. A leader who tells you what you want to hear? Or...

2. A leader who states honest opinions and intentions—which you disagree with vehemently?

This question sounds simpler than it really is. Take your time.

ALL HAT AND NO CATTLE

Respect, popularity, influence, and trust can all be won with image and word tricks. But they can also be won by simply being direct and honest, even though many people today believe that it's impossible to be who we really are and still be acceptable.

Real cowboys have a saying about people who are nothing but image. They call them "all hat and no cattle." These people talk big and make big promises, but they aren't around when you need them. They have a great image (a hat) but no substance (cattle).

As we pay higher and higher prices to image-makers to recreate our looks, our speech, and our personality, we tend to get more and more confused. We become image people watching other image people on a TV screen, each believing in the image of the other, knowing that our own image was built by a PR person or a plastic surgeon.

In the public schools of Toronto, Canada, "media" is a required subject. Students learn how those images on the screen manipulate our thinking. They learn about camera angles that make people look bigger than life, about sound bites that make people sound better than they really are. They learn how to watch and listen in a questioning way. They learn how to spot image without substance.

"All hat and no cattle" might be fine for a time. But eventually, many people get hungry for something more real. Is image enough for you?

CHAPTER 9

YOU ARE AN AGENT OF TRUTH

WIDENING YOUR TRUTH

Described below are 10 notable Americans. Can you identify the one thing they all have in common? (Widening your truth is a good way to combat lies.)

1. ***Bert Williams:*** W.C. Fields called him the greatest comic in the world.

2. ***Granville T. Woods:*** Patented the galvanic battery and electric relay switches which make stoplights work.

3. ***Lewis Latimer:*** Co-invented with Thomas Edison the carbon filament for the electric light bulb.

4. ***Dr. Charles Drew:*** Pioneered the process for storing blood plasma.

5. ***James Bland:*** Composed nearly 700 musical works.

6. ***Percy Julian:*** Researched drugs to treat glaucoma.

7. ***James Beckworth:*** This explorer and scout rode with Kit Carson and discovered the pass through the Sierra Nevada mountains through which thousands traveled to search for gold in California.

8. ***Benjamin Banneker:*** Manufactured one of the first clocks in America.

9. ***Matthew Henson:*** With Admiral Robert E. Peary, he conquered the top of the world in 1909.

10. ***C.J. Walker:*** One of the first American women to become a millionaire.

Find the answer on page **158**.

WHEN REALITY SHIFTS

You are standing on an Earth you have always known to be solid and unshakable. Suddenly it starts to move—it's an earthquake! What do you do? How do you react? The reality you have counted on has let you down. It has given way beneath your feet.

This may be how you felt as you read through *The First Honest Book about Lies*. Much of what you have counted on may have shifted before your eyes. You may be wondering, "Is everything a lie? Can nothing be trusted?" The truth is that the world *is* full of lies. And, just as people learn to deal with earthquakes, you must learn to deal with this fundamental truth.

At first you may feel helpless. But you aren't helpless. There is much you can do to be comfortable in a world of lies— and there is much you can do to add to the truth in the world.

FOUR WAYS TO LIVE IN A WORLD OF LIES

1. Consider the alternative.

Think about how it would be to live in a world of absolute truth.

- You would sacrifice much of your privacy. People could ask you whatever they wanted, and you would have to answer. You couldn't hear or tell a secret.

- There would be no amusement parks, no illusions, no fiction. Imagine what would happen to movies and TV programs.

- Forget about figures of speech. Similes and metaphors wouldn't be allowed. You couldn't exaggerate or tell a tall tale.

- You would have to live without social lies—the pleasant, easy exchanges like "How are you?" "I'm fine."

How else would absolute truth affect your everyday life?

2. Realize that the truth almost always comes out...eventually.

As Abraham Lincoln once said, "It is true that you may fool all the people some of the time; you can even fool some of the people all the time; but you can't fool all of the people all the time." Truth has a way of outlasting lies. Lies may be the blossoms that show in the spring, but truth is the roots that live through many long winters.

Thomas Paine was an American patriot whose booklet, *Common Sense,* inspired the American Revolution. Paine saw many truths long before his famous peers did. While Thomas Jefferson was still a slave holder, Paine was speaking out against slavery. While Abigail Adams had to remind her husband, John (the second President of the United States), not to forget about women's rights, Paine was busy making others aware that women were the forgotten citizens in the new government. Paine also spoke and wrote about animal rights, which were of little or no concern to other leaders of his time.

Things that were painfully obvious to Thomas Paine were invisible to most people of his time. He must have been frustrated to see otherwise intelligent individuals accept such lies as the institution of slavery and the inferiority of women. But instead of feeling sorry for himself, he tried his best to make others see the truth. And bit by bit over the years, the truth about slavery and women's rights finally emerged.

It may take years or centuries before some truths come out, but they *will* come out. Lies don't last forever because they are usually told for selfish reasons. The truth, on the other hand, is told for its own sake. It is repeated by patient, persistent, and wise people for generations until it is finally heard.

If you feel frustrated when you can't convince others to see the truth, keep trying. Tell yourself that the truth *will* get through, and your voice is important in making it happen.

"For truth there is no deadline."

—Heywood Broun

3. Don't be a victim of lies.

Sometimes people fall for a lie because they are greedy. They think they really can get something for nothing. Sometimes people are too lazy to ask questions and gather facts. They would rather live with the way things are than work for change.

Even if you aren't greedy or lazy, you will sometimes be fooled or tricked. Rather than feel sorry for yourself, use these occasions to learn about yourself. Try to figure out what things are most likely to deceive you. Are you taken in by charming personalities? By get-rich-quick schemes? By flattery? By statistics?

4. Remember that lying has been around forever.

Despite this fact, life goes on. The world goes on. You go on. Somehow, in some way, we all figure out how to live with lies.

"The truth is great, and shall prevail When none cares whether it prevail or not."

—Coventry Patmore

HOW TO TELL WHEN YOU'RE BEING LIED TO

Through the centuries, people have fought lies by trying to identify liars. A papyrus from 900 B.C. offers this description of a liar:

> He does not answer questions, or gives evasive answers; he speaks nonsense, rubs the great toe along the ground and shivers; he rubs the roots of his hair with his fingers.

In the ancient Orient, a person suspected of lying was given dry rice to chew and spit out. If he was honest, he could easily spit out the rice. If he was lying, he couldn't—his fear of being found out dried up his saliva. Of course, this technique assumes that all liars are fearful, which may or may not be true.

Arabian Bedouins tested suspected liars by having them lick a hot iron. The dry-mouthed liars burned their tongues; the truth-tellers (or non-fearful liars) were not hurt.

Today, certain behaviors are commonly believed to reveal that someone is lying. They include stammering, using vague descriptions or elaborate explanations, offering too many excuses, or pausing for long periods. In fact, these behaviors aren't always good indicators. There are other, more reliable signs you can stay alert for.

• •

CAUTION
None of these signs is *proof* that someone is lying. But they can alert you to keep your ears and eyes open. In each case, consider the situation and review what you know about the person you think may be lying to you. Gather as much information as you can, then weigh it carefully before making up your mind.

• •

- **The eyes.** Some people avoid eye contact when they are lying. They get "shifty eyed."

- **The smile.** People smile less when they are lying. Or they try to cover up their lie by forcing themselves to smile.

How can you tell the difference between a real smile and a forced smile? A real smile makes wrinkles around the eyes; a forced smile doesn't. A forced smile lasts longer than a real one. A forced smile is stronger on the left side of a right-handed person, and on the right side of a left-handed person.

- **The hands.** Liars touch their faces more often than truth-tellers to relieve some of the anxiety they feel while lying. Practiced liars know to keep their hands hidden. (Of course, this assumes that liars feel anxious when they lie, which may or may not be true.)

- **The voice.** Liars may sigh. Their voices may rise, as if their sentences end with question marks. Their voices may sound inappropriate for the surroundings or the occasion— too eager or too restrained, too casual or too urgent.

- **Mismatches.** Does he say, "I love you," in a sing-song voice? Does she claim, "I am so happy for you," in a flat, lifeless voice? Are gentle words paired with angry gestures, or sad eyes with a happy voice?

- **Motive.** What, if anything, does the person have to gain from lying to you? Is there money involved? Does the person think you want something from him or her?

- **Reasonableness.** Does what the person is saying make sense to you? Or do you have to stretch your imagination to believe your ears?

- **Rightness.** Think of your favorite song, performed by your favorite artist. You know how it's supposed to sound. If it's a little too fast or slow, a little too high or low, you know immediately that it isn't "right."

You can learn to tell when someone's words aren't "right." You've had enough experience with friends, family, teachers, and others to have a good idea of how people typically act and sound in given situations. Use what you know to stay close to the truth.

- **Your gut feelings.** According to Martin G. Groder, M.D. and psychiatrist, gut feelings originate in the right side of the brain, not the "gut." The visual right side of the brain stores past experiences like a videotape stores images. It compares new experiences with the stored experiences. When a new experience doesn't "fit," you get a "gut feeling"—for example, "This person is lying." You're not sure how you know; you just know. If someone asked you why, you probably couldn't explain.

Trust your gut feelings. Sometimes they are the only "evidence" you have to go on.

DETECTING LIES: SOCIETY TRIES

- In 17th-century Salem, Massachusetts, officials used to ask suspected witches (usually women), "Are you a witch?" If the person answered "no," the officials would tie her hands and feet and throw her into deep water. If she drowned, this was proof that she had been telling the truth—she wasn't a witch. But if she lived, this meant that she had been lying—she was a witch. In Salem at that time, witches were burned at the stake. Clearly it was best to avoid being asked if you were a witch.

- Ben Franklin studied American and English phonetics. He concluded that the nonsense syllables "Uh-huh" for "yes" and "Unh-uh" for "no" could help to detect English spies, because the English couldn't distinguish between them. Franklin suggested that these syllables be used as passwords for American encampments, and Congress recommended the idea to George Washington. But Washington himself couldn't distinguish between "uh-huh" and "unh-uh."

- Many people have tried to concoct "truth serums." Scopolamine, popular during the 1930's, can help people relax and talk more freely, but it can't keep them from making false statements. Sodium pentathol is another questionable "truth drug."

- During World War II, people entering American camps were questioned about batting averages and comic-strip characters. The military police reasoned that "real Americans" would know the answers. In the Pacific Islands, Orientals were ordered to say the word "lalapaloosa" to reveal if they were Chinese or Japanese. The Americans reasoned that because Chinese say their R's like L's, and the Japanese say their L's like R's, this test would expose any enemy spies.

- The first lie detector was designed by Italian scientist Cesare Lombroso in 1895. Lombroso's machine measured changes in a suspect's pulse and blood pressure. In 1914, Vittorio Benussi invented the pneumograph, which measured changes in a suspect's breathing caused by guilt feelings. William Marston helped to develop the galvanometer, which measured changes in skin resistance. In 1921, John A. Larson invented the polygraph, which continuously recorded a person's blood pressure, pulse, and respiration. Leonarde Keeler introduced an advanced version of the polygraph in 1949.

"It is always the best policy to speak the truth, unless you are an exceptionally good liar."

—Jerome K. Jerome

Polygraphs are still in use today, but experts disagree about their effectiveness. These devices can only measure a person's guilt, anger, fear, or resentment about being tested. If a suspect isn't guilty, angry, fearful, or resentful—or nervous—then they just don't work. It is now illegal for employers to use polygraphs on their employees because the results are so questionable. Their overall accuracy rate may be as low as 25 percent.

HOW TO LET YOUR TRUTHFULNESS SHOW

Have you ever told the truth, but nobody believed you? Maybe it's the *way* you told it. Some words and phrases make you *seem* less believable, even when you're being completely honest. Some ways of talking make you *seem* less trustworthy, as if you've got something to hide.

- Don't use wishy-washy phrases like "It seems…," "Perhaps…," "Sort of…," and "I think…"

- Don't over-use words like "very," "really," "actually," and "honestly."

- Don't end all of your sentences with a question mark. (Do you know people who do this? They make a statement, and their voices rise at the end? As if they're waiting for you to agree with them? But all it does is drive you crazy?)

- Don't appear to be seeking approval. We all want other people to like us, but when we make that our top priority, we compromise our believability.

- Don't use "umh" and "uh." (Those, uh, syllables, umh, uh, make you sound, uh, as if you're not sure of what you're, uh, talking about.)

How can you reveal your truthfulness? Stand up (or sit up) straight. Look the other person in the eye. Think about what you want to say. Then tell it like it is!

WHAT TRAPS YOU INTO LIES?

When are you most likely to lie, either to yourself or to others? When lying is easier than telling the truth? When lying helps you to keep up appearances? When lying lets you avoid responsibility?

Find out by asking yourself the three sets of questions that follow. Record your answers on a separate sheet of paper. Be honest with yourself! By discovering why and when you lie, you'll get to know yourself better. The better you know yourself, the closer you'll come to becoming an agent of truth.

Taking It Easy

1. Which would you rather watch?

  A. A four-part TV series spread out over four nights

  B. A half-hour sitcom

2. Which would you rather win?

  A. A $500 savings bond you can cash in 10 years

  B. $100 in cash you can spend now

3. Which would you rather attend?

  A. A baseball game

  B. A basketball game

4. How would you rather travel to a new place?

  A. By automobile

  B. By jet

5. Which would you rather play?

  A. Chess

  B. Checkers

6. How would you prefer to communicate with a friend in another city?

  A. By letter

  B. By telephone

7. You get to have one chocolate bar per week. How will you eat it?

  A. One square a day, to make it last

  B. All at once

8. You've just bought your best friend an exciting gift. What will you do?

  A. Wait to give it to your friend on the next important occasion

  B. Give it to your friend right away

9. You have to build a model. Which will you use?
   A. A pre-painted, snap-together kit
   B. A glue-together kit you paint yourself

10. Which would you rather read?
    A. A novel
    B. A short story

11. You have to do a project. How will you go about it?
    A. Neatly and carefully, taking your time
    B. As fast as you can

12. When would you rather do your homework?
    A. Right after school
    B. Later, after dinner and your favorite TV shows

Scoring: Add up your A's and B's.

Interpreting your score: If you have eight or more B's, you tend to take the short-term view over the long-term view. You do what's easiest at the moment, without thinking about the consequences. You like quick answers and immediate gratification. This can lead to self-lies and excuses ("I'll do it later"..."It's not my fault that I didn't finish that project"... "I didn't know it would take so long").

What you can do: Practice being patient. Stop making excuses. Aim for long-term rewards.

Looking Good

1. Which would you rather watch?
   A. Your school's homecoming game
   B. The playoffs of a sport you enjoy but your friends don't like

2. Which would you rather win?
   A. A popularity contest
   B. An essay contest

3. Which would you rather attend?
   A. A party
   B. A meeting with a famous person—but you can't tell anyone about it afterward

4. How would you rather travel to a new place?
   A. By limousine
   B. By jet, but in coach class

5. Which would you rather play?
   A. The latest, most popular board game
   B. Chess

DINE & DANCE

6. How would you prefer to communicate with a friend in another city?

A. In the latest slang

B. In proper English

7. You are served a plate of spaghetti at a dinner party. How will you eat it?

A. The same way you would eat it if you were home alone

B. Twirl it neatly on your fork and try not to slurp

8. You've just bought your best friend an exciting gift. What will you do?

A. Give it to your friend in front of other people

B. Give it to your friend anonymously or one-on-one

9. You have to build a model. Which will you use?

A. Glitter and glass

B. Plaster and paint

10. Which would you rather read?

A. A current bestseller

B. A book about your favorite hobby

11. You have to do a project. How will you do it?

A. In a way you think will please other people

B. In a way that meets your own standards

12. Which would you rather do?

A. Go along with the crowd and do something that bores you

B. Do something you enjoy, even if you have to do it alone

Scoring: Add up your A's and B's.

Interpreting your score: If you have eight or more A's, you tend to be motivated by the need for outside approval. You worry about how others will see you and what they will think of you. This leads to self-lies and rationalizations ("I really need those $150 shoes"…"I'll go along with the crowd just this once").

What you can do: Ask yourself, "Am I doing this because it's good for me, or because it looks good to other people?" In fact, being "good for you" and "looking good" aren't necessarily opposites. Many people admire those who have the courage to follow their convictions. At first, you may attract some teasing and name-calling, but in time, people will come to respect your integrity.

Who's Responsible?

1. Which would you rather be responsible for taking care of?

A. A puppy

B. A house plant

2. Which would you rather win?

    A. A seat on the student council

    B. Dinner at a local restaurant

3. Which would you rather attend?

    A. A quiz show—as a contestant

    B. A quiz show—as an audience member

4. How would you rather travel to a new place?

    A. Drive

    B. Ride

5. Which would you rather play?

    A. Charades

    B. Go Fish

6. How would you prefer to communicate with a friend in another city?

    A. In person

    B. By telephone

7. You and a friend decide to go out to dinner together. Which would you rather be?

    A. The person who chooses the restaurant

    B. The person who goes along with the other person's choice

8. You've just bought your best friend an exciting gift. What will you do?

    A. Wrap it and deliver it personally

    B. Have the store wrap it and deliver it

9. You have to build a model. Which will you use?

    A. A highly detailed model with hundreds of pieces

    B. A quick and easy kit

10. Which would you rather read?

    A. A how-to book about something you want or need to learn

    B. An escapist fantasy

11. You have to do a project. How will you do it?

    A. By yourself, from beginning to end, personally handling every detail

    B. You'll start it, but then you'll find someone else to finish it

12. You made a mistake. What will you do?

    A. Accept the consequences and try to make it right

    B. Ignore the consequences

Scoring: Add up your A's and B's.

Interpreting your score: If you have eight or more B's, you tend to avoid taking responsibility for your words and actions. This leads to excuses and blaming ("I didn't do it"…"I couldn't help it"…"It wasn't my fault").

What you can do: Stop making excuses. Stop blaming other people. Realize that you, and only you, are responsible for your words and actions. Recognize that your words and actions have consequences.

NINE WAYS TO ATTRACT THE TRUTH

You can't force other people to tell you the truth, but you can make it more likely that they will. You can become the kind of person it's easy to be truthful with.

1. *Become known as a truthful person.* Wouldn't you rather be truthful with people who are honest with you?

2. *Keep secrets.* If someone shares a confidence with you, keep it confidential. Make this one of your personal trademarks, and people will trust you with their truths. (Exceptions: when a friend is in danger; when the potential consequences of keeping a secret are worse than telling a trusted adult.)

3. *Be careful how you use other people's truths.* Example: A friend confides that he is afraid of spiders. Later, you make fun of his fear in front of a crowd of your peers. Or you use it to get back at him the next time he makes you angry. Your friend will wish he had never been truthful with you in the first place—and he won't repeat his mistake.

4. *Don't be critical.* If sharing the truth with you is an unpleasant experience—if you always respond with criticism—people will stop doing it.

5. *Resist the urge to give advice unless it is asked for.* Are you likely to share the truth with someone who immediately replies, "Here's what you should do" or "Here's what you should have done"?

6. *Don't be overly sensitive.* It's hard to be truthful with someone whose feelings are always getting hurt, or who interprets every little remark as a personal insult.

7. *Keep an open mind, and be willing to change your mind.* If you're set in your ways, no one will tell you truths that don't fit with your beliefs. Instead, be receptive to new facts and information. Seek out both sides of any issue that's important to you. You're most likely to be misled when all you know is one side.

"What everybody echoes as true today, may turn out to be falsehood tomorrow, mere smoke of opinion."

—Thoreau

8. **Don't jump to conclusions.** Suspend your judgment until most of the facts are in. Ask questions to gather more facts. Wait to make a decision until you feel ready.

9. **Be a good listener.** People are more likely to tell you the truth when you give them your full attention without interrupting.

PUTTING THINGS IN PERSPECTIVE

Now that you've become a living lie detector, you may be wondering, "How can I be skeptical without becoming cynical? How can I be trusting without being gullible?"

The word *skeptical* is from a Greek tradition of philosophy which encouraged doubting and questioning. Skeptics believed that the truth was not knowable, and that judgment should be suspended. They believed in waiting until all the facts were in before deciding on an ultimate truth. At the same time, they realized that all the facts could never be in. This made them seek out even more facts to get closer to the truth.

FOR INQUIRING MINDS

Are you skeptical of so-called "news stories" about UFO's, psychics, ESP, faith healers, spoon benders, and more? Then you might enjoy the *Skeptical Inquirer*. This quarterly journal is dedicated to fighting nonsense. Written by scientists, it investigates and exposes pseudoscientific theories and claims. Ask your library to subscribe, or write to:

Skeptical Inquirer
Box 703
Buffalo, NY 14226.
Or call toll-free 1-800-634-1610.

To the philosopher Descartes, doubt was the reason for existence. You may know his famous saying, *Cogito, Ergo Sum*—"I think, therefore I am." For people like Descartes, lies served the purpose of making them think and investigate.

"The cynic is the one who knows the price of everything and the value of nothing."

—Oscar Wilde

If lies can make you think, then maybe they aren't so bad after all. If they lead to new discoveries, maybe they're good for you.

Another group of philosophers called the Cynics were even more skeptical than the Skeptics. They believed that every action was motivated by self-interest alone. They were suspicious of everyone. They tended to be gloomy and distrustful.

Diogenes was a cynic who rejected material things and wandered the streets of Athens in tattered clothes. One day, when the sun was high in the sky, a friend met him. Diogenes was carrying a lighted lantern and seemed to be looking for something. The friend followed Diogenes for about an hour and finally said, "You do not seem to be finding what you are seeking, good Diogenes. May I ask just what it is?" Diogenes replied, "I am searching for an honest man." Then he continued on.

Diogenes may have missed much of the truth of life, which was there before him all the time. The truth of sunlight, the truth of friendship, and the truth of learning for its own sake are all worth looking for. Rather than spending his time searching for an honest man, Diogenes could have become one himself. He could have found what he was seeking in his own reflection.

As an agent of truth, you can influence others and make your voice heard. You can be on the lookout for lies and speak out against them. You can make your own choices and develop your own integrity. You can ask questions and expose the lies you find.

But don't ask the impossible of yourself or other people. Realize that every day, new facts are added to what you know as "reality." Each fact brings you closer to the truth. Each has the potential to replace a lie with enlightenment.

Find honesty by being honest, and you'll find your truth in your mirror.

TRUTH #8:
YOU HAVE TO FIND YOUR OWN TRUTH.

FINDING YOUR TRUTH

In the end, it's you who must decide what your own truth is, which lies are too big to take, and which truths are too big to ignore.

Make a list of the truths and lies in your life. Narrow it down to your seven most important insights into the subject.

The following list was written by Philip Higgins, a young writer who's a senior at George Fox College in Newberg, Oregon. How does your list compare?

ONE:

The biggest lie: "I Love You."

(Corollaries: "Trust Me." "I Did It for You.")

TWO:

Number One can also be the biggest truth. Be wary.

THREE:

There are two kinds of truth: the truth of our perceptions/beliefs, and the truth that exists in spite of us.

FOUR:

When we tell the "truth" to others, we most often are lying to ourselves.

FIVE:

When we lie to others, we often reveal the truth to (about) ourselves.

SIX:

Friendships/relationships are based on mutually accepted lies.

SEVEN:

A very, very big lie is that there is an "us" and a "them."

"Truth is said to lie at the bottom of a well, for the very reason, perhaps, that whoever looks down in search of her sees his own image at the bottom."

—James Russell Lowell

ANSWERS TO PROBLEMS, QUESTIONS, AND QUIZZES

ANSWERS TO "TRUE OR FALSE?" ON PAGE 39

1. **FALSE.** In fact, there are tons of diamonds around the world, and the only reason diamonds are expensive is because one company, the De Beers Mining Company of South Africa, controls 80% of the world's supply.

2. **FALSE.** In 1938, De Beers began an advertising campaign to link diamonds to "love." In 1948, the company's ads showed young lovers on a honeymoon with the words, "A Diamond Is Forever." Sales soared from $23 million in 1939 to more than $2.1 billion in 1979. People were convinced that they "needed" diamonds to prove their love. Now it's customary to give diamond engagement rings—but the custom is only about 50 years old. (Today's ads from De Beers encourage men to spend "three months' salary" on a diamond engagement ring. That's a lot of money!)

ANSWERS TO "TRUE OR FALSE? ON PAGE 43

1. **FALSE.** Your body can absorb only so much Vitamin A. Stuffing yourself with carrots can't improve your eyesight. But too much carrot-eating *can* turn your skin an orange color.

2. **FALSE.** The iron in spinach is supposed to make you strong, but just eating foods rich in iron isn't enough. Even if it were, spinach has only modest amounts of iron.

3. **FALSE.** "Even large amounts of chocolate have not clinically exacerbated [made worse] acne," doctors wrote in the *Journal of the American Medical Association* as long ago as 1978.

SCORING TIPS FOR "A SELF-LIE TEST" ON PAGE 50

The tendency is for people to judge themselves at extremes—to see themselves as better or worse than the "average" person. If you believe you are kinder, busier, and more sensitive than "most people," then you are probably like "most people." Somebody must not be telling the whole truth.

Give this test to as many people as you can. Compare your responses. Do you all see yourselves as different from "most people"? What does that tell you?

P.S. Horoscope writers count on this human tendency to resist being labeled "average." They can say, "As a Libra, you tend to be more diplomatic than most people...." And most Libras will say to themselves, "Yes, that describes me!"

ANSWERS TO THE PUZZLE ON PAGE 71

Fats always tell the truth. Targa is not a Fat because he would have to truthfully answer, "I am a Fat." He is also not a Skinny, because Skinnies always lie and Targa has just told the truth. Targa must be a Muscle.

String says, "I am not a Muscle." This is true, because Targa is the Muscle. String therefore can't be a Skinny because Skinnies always lie. String is a Fat.

Braun is a Skinny, because that's all that's left.

And Clue, Sam's friend, is a Fat, because truth-telling String says so!

ANSWERS TO "STUDIES SHOW..." ON PAGE 76

1. **B.** Ask if the subjects were rats, cats, lizards, or people. This particular study was done on hamsters. Tests done on rodents don't necessarily translate directly to humans.

2. **B.** Maybe only five people were tested. Maybe they were all related to the inventor of Brand A.

3. **A.** In this case, Quaker Oats paid for the study. If other studies confirm that oat bran is good for you, then B would also be correct.

4. **B.** A *retrospective* study is not as reliable as a *prospective* one, in which researchers observe and control the various parts of the story as it is in progress.

5. **B.** If the jogger-subjects were volunteers and the non-jogger subjects were non-volunteers, this might make a difference. Perhaps the volunteers looked younger because they knew they were being studied and were more careful about their appearance—not because they had a "healthy glow" from jogging.

   Another question you might ask: Younger than who?

TIP: If you truly doubt the results of any study, you may want to wait for confirmation from a large national organization, such as the American Heart Association or the American Cancer Society.

ANSWERS TO "SHOULD YOU TAKE THIS JOB, OR SHOVE IT?" ON PAGE 80

1. Start by figuring the *mean*:

   $45,000 + $3,000 + $1,000 + $500 + $500 = $50,000

   $50,000 divided by 5 = $10,000

   CONCLUSION: The personnel manager was telling the truth. Take the job!

2. Next, figure the *mode*:

   The mode is the number that appears most often: $500.

   CONCLUSION: The president was telling the truth. Shove the job!

3. Finally, figure the *median*:

The median is the number that falls exactly in the middle, with two higher and two lower: $1,000.

CONCLUSION: The company spokesperson was telling the truth. Take it...no, wait, shove it...no, wait....

TIP: Ask the personnel manager what *your* salary will be. Then make your decision based on that number.

ANSWERS TO "TRUE OR FALSE?" ON PAGE 89

George Washington:

A. FALSE. This story was made up by a man who wanted to make money from writing inexpensive books about American heroes. The writer, named Weems, said, "You have a great deal of money lying in the bones of old George."

B. FALSE. This story was made up by drunken Continental soldiers.

C. FALSE. This story was made up, probably by George Washington himself. He often exaggerated, making conditions seem much worse than they really were so he could get more money for his troops from Congress.

D. TRUE. It seems that George Washington could tell a lie after all. But he couldn't spell one.

Betsy Ross:

A. FALSE. Betsy Ross did not stitch the first American flag.

B. FALSE. She did not have anything to do with designing it, either. Congress gives credit to Francis Hopkinson for the flag design.

C. TRUE. He made up the whole story.

ANSWERS TO "TRUE OR FALSE?" ON PAGE 90

All six of these statements are FALSE. You can find hundreds more like them in a book by Paul Dickson and Joseph C. Goulden called *There Are Alligators in Our Sewers & Other American Credos: A Collection of Bunk, Nonsense, and Fables We Believe* (New York: Delacorte Press, 1983).

ANSWERS TO "TRUE OR FALSE?" ON PAGE 93

1. FALSE.

2. FALSE.

3. TRUE.

4. FALSE.

5. TRUE.

6. FALSE. But just to keep the peace with your parents, you may decide to wear your jacket when it's cold outside. (Besides, you'll be more comfortable.)

7. FALSE. Actually, this is true and not true. Practice improves your performance, but the actual improvement comes during the resting phase, during which your learning is "cemented." See for yourself. Repeat the words "toy boat" over and over again. You'll soon hear your performance go downhill as the words become meaningless sounds. Wait a little, try again, and you'll sound as good as when you started.

8. TRUE. Babies who are not held and touched tend to lose weight and become less healthy.

9. FALSE. But it certainly seems easier to read with good light.

10. FALSE. But for many years, people didn't eat tomatoes because it was widely believed that they were poisonous.

Alfie Kohn, author of *You Know What They Say...The Truth about Popular Beliefs*, looked for scientific support for certain commonly accepted "truths" such as these. He found out that many of the things we accept because "they say so" are simply not true.

How do you think some of these ideas got started? Why do people tend to believe them? Is it because they sound true, or is it because they have been repeated so often?

ANSWERS TO "HOW TO NEVER TELL A LIE" ON PAGE 133

1. Killing (in war)

2. Killing (the crime)

3. Death (in a hospital)

4. Used clothes

5. Short

6. Used car

7. Custodian (janitor)

ANSWER TO "WIDENING YOUR TRUTH" ON PAGE 137

All 10 were African Americans.

You have probably heard of Kit Carson, Thomas Edison, and Admiral Peary, some of the people these notable Americans worked with. But how many of their names fell within your awareness of the truth of the past?

BIBLIOGRAPHY

Atkinson, Richard C., Rita L. Atkinson, and Ernest R. Hilgard. *Introduction to Psychology.* Sixth edition. New York: Harcourt Brace Jovanovich, Inc., 1975.

Ayer, Alfred Jules. *Language Truth and Logic.* Second edition. New York: Dover Publications Inc., 1952.

Bandler, Richard, and John Grinder. *Trance-formations.* Utah: Real People Press, 1981.

Barry, Sheila Anne. *Super-colossal Book of Puzzles, Tricks and Games.* New York: Sterling Publishing Co., Inc., 1978.

Berlitz, Charles. *Native Tongues.* New York: Grosset and Dunlap, 1982.

Bozzi, Vincent. "Good-looking Lies." *Psychology Today* (January 1986): 12-13.

Brown, Roger. *Words and Things.* Second printing. Illinois: The Free Press, 1959.

Brunvand, Jan Harold. *The Vanishing Hitchhiker.* New York: W.W. Norton and Company, 1981.

Burnam, Tom. *More Misinformation.* New York: Lippincott & Crowell, 1980.

Burnam, Tom. *The Dictionary of Misinformation.* New York: Ballantine Books, 1975.

Calero, Henry H., and Gerard I. Nirenberg. *Metatalk.* New York: Simon and Schuster, 1981.

Campbell, Joseph. *Myths to Live By.* Eleventh printing. New York: Bantam Books, 1988.

Church, Joseph, and L. Joseph Stone. *Childhood and Adolescence.* Second edition. New York: Random House, 1968.

Darling, Edward, and Ashley Montagu. *The Prevalence of Nonsense.* New York: Harper & Row, Publishers, Inc., 1967.

Dickson, Paul, and Joseph C. Goulden. *There Are Alligators in Our Sewers and Other American Credos: A Collection of Bunk, Nonsense, and Fables We Believe.* New York: Delacorte Press, 1983.

A Dictionary of Philosophy. Revised second edition. New York: St. Martin's Press, 1979.

Dushkin, David A. *Psychology Today: An Introduction.* New York: Communications/Reasearch/Machines Inc., 1970.

Elwood, Ann, Carol Orsag, and Sindey Solomon. *Macmillan Illustrated Almanac for Kids.* New York: Macmillan Publishing Company, 1981.

Ferguson, Marilyn. *The Brain Revolution.* New York: Bantam Books, 1975.

Fulghum, Robert. *It Was on Fire When I Lay Down on It.* New York: Ivy Books, 1989.

Geivitz, James. *Looking at Ourselves.* Boston: Little, Brown, and Company, 1976.

Goldberg, M. Hirsh. *The Blunder Book*. New York: William Morrow and Company, Inc., 1984.

Guillen, Michael A. "Life as a Lottery." *Psychology Today* (October 1983): 59-61.

Hamilton, Edith. *Mythology*. New York: Mentor Books, 1942.

Hampden-Turner, Charles. *Maps of the Mind*. New York: Macmillan Publishing Company, 1981.

Harris, Marvin. *Cows, Pigs, Wars, and Witches*. Vintage Books edition, 1989. Random House, Inc., 1974.

Hirsch, E.D. Jr., Joseph Kett, and James Trefil. *The Dictionary of Cultural Literacy*. Boston: Houghton Miffin Company, 1988.

Hoffer, Eric. *The True Believer*. New York: Time Incorporated, 1963.

Hoffman, Mark S. *The World Almanac 1991*. New York: Pharos Books, 1990.

Hofstadter, Douglas R. *Metamagical Themas*. New York: Macmillan Publishing Company, 1981.

Horn, Jack C. "Engendering Excuses." *Psychology Today* (January 1986): 12.

Huff, Darrell. *How to Lie with Statistics*. New York: W.W. Norton & Company, Inc., 1954.

Jacobson, Viola E., and Samuel E. Lowe. *Fifty Famous Stories*. Wisconsin: Whitman Publishing Company, 1920.

Jellison, Jerald M. *I'm Sorry I Didn't Mean to and Other Lies We Love to Tell*. New York: Chatham Square Press, 1977.

Jordan, Nick. "When to Lie to Yourself." *Psychology Today* (June 1989): 24.

Key, Wilson Bryan. *Media Sexploitation*. New Jersey: Prentice-Hall Inc., 1976.

King, Richard A., and Clifford T. Morgan. *Introduction to Psychology*. Third edition. New York: McGraw-Hill Book Company, 1966.

Kohn, Alfie. *You Know What They Say...The Truth about Popular Beliefs*. New York: Harper-Collins, 1990.

Lederer, Richard. *Crazy English*. New York: Pocket Books, 1990.

Lloyd, Kenneth, and Donald Moine. *Unlimited Selling Power*. New Jersey: Prentice-Hall Inc., 1990.

Lutz, William. *Doublespeak*. New York: Harper & Row, 1989.

McCutcheson, Marc. *The Compass in Your Nose and Other Astonishing Facts about Humans*. California: Jeremy P. Tarcher, Inc., 1989.

McGinniss, Joe. *The Selling of the President 1968*. New York: Trident Press, 1969.

Marsh, Dave. *50 Ways to Fight Censorship*. New York: Thunder's Mouth Press, 1991.

Molloy, John T. *Dress for Success*. New York: Warner Books, Inc., 1975.

Molloy, John T. *The New Dress for Success*. New York: Warner Books, Inc., 1988.

Moss, Ruth J. "Candidate Camera." *Psychology Today* (December 1986): 20.

Packard, Vance. *The Hidden Persuaders*. Great Britain: Pelican Books, 1957.

Packard, Vance. *The Status Seekers*. New York: Pocket Books, 1959.

Paulos, John Allen. *Innumeracy*. Vintage Books edition, 1990. New York: Hill and Wang: 1988.

Poundstone, William. *Big Secrets*. New York: Quill, 1983.

Ross, Edward Alsworth. *Social Psychology*. New York: The Macmillan Company, 1912.

Rounds, Glen. *Ol' Paul, the Mighty Logger*. Seventh printing. U.S.: Holiday House, Inc., 1949.

Royko, Mike. "Sensitivity Can Become Offensive." *The Oregonian* (4 June 1990): B7.

Ruby, Lionel, and Robert E. Yarber. *The Art of Making Sense.* Third edition. New York: J.P. Lippincott Comany, 1974.

Ruchlis, Hy. *How Do You Know It's True? Discovering the Difference between Science & Superstition*. New York: Prometheus Books, 1991.

Sacks, Oliver. *The Man Who Mistook His Wife for a Hat*. New York: Summit Books, 1985.

Schudson, Michael. "The Giving of Gifts." *Psychology Today* (December 1986): 27-29.

Shenkman, Richard. *I Love Paul Revere, Whether He Rode or Not*. New York: HarperCollins Publishers, 1991.

Sidis, Boris. *The Psychology of Suggestion*. New York: D. Appleton and Company, 1898.

Tuleja, Thaddeus. *The Cat's Pajamas*. New York: Fawcett Columbine, 1987.

Tuleja, Thaddeus. *Fabulous Fallacies*, New York: Harmony Books, 1982.

Weinberger, Norman M., and Richard E. Whalen. *Psychobiology*. California: W.H. Freeman and Company, 1967.

INDEX

F

Fabrication, as history, 2
Fact
    denying, 37
    vs. opinion, 8
Family agreement, no-fault, 48
Family myths. *See under* Myths
Far Side (cartoon), 27
Feelings. *See* Emotions
Figures of speech, 138
Focus, and truth, 19-20
Food, falsehoods, 43-44
Franklin, Benjamin, 91, 142
Free choice, 85
Freedom of Information Act, 127-
    128, 131
Freedom of speech, 95
Friends, 64
Fulghum, Robert, 61-62

G

Gallup, George, 83
Gallup polls, 83
Gangs, 65-66
Garisto, Robert, 72
Gergen, David, 27
Ghostwriting, 40, 41
Gift-giving, 67-69
Gifted people, and imposter
    phenomenon, 52
Gilbert, Melissa, 52
Good old days, illusion of, 21-22
Gossip, 60
    as myth, 96
Greed, and lies, 139
Gregorian calendar, 42
Griffith, Melanie, 52
Groder, Martin, 141
Groener, Andrea, 99
Gulf War, 131, 134

H

Hair dyes, 37
Hands, as revealing lie, 141
Havel, Vaclav, 70
Headlines, misleading, 130
Health, 37
Hearing, sense of
    as lying, 11
    and pitch of baby's cry, 12
    and skin sensitivity, 12
Hemingway, Ernest, 91
Henson, Matthew, 137
Hidden meanings, 26-27
Higgens, Philip, 151
Hiroshima, Japan, 90

History

History
    absolute, 5
    fabrication as, 2
    illusion of past as better, 21-22
    vs. lies, 5
    and myth, 89-92, 101-102
Hitler, Adolf, 125, 126
Holidays, 6
Honesty
    and lies, 8, 9
    personal standards for, 2
    and power, 59
    total, 61
Hoover, Herbert, 128
Huckleberry Finn (Twain), 93, 95
Humor, and contest, 27
Hundredth Monkey, The (Watson),
    84-86
Hussein, Saddam, 126

I

Ideas, selling of, 105-106
Illusion
    afterimages as, 30-32
    ambiguous figures as, 16-19
    and comparison, 22-26
    figure/ground, 16
    and philosophy/physiology, 13
    proofreader's error, 28-29
    vs. truth, 13, 15-16, 138
Image, 145-146
    public relations as, 122
    selling of, 105-106, 116
    vs. substance, 136
Influence, 8
Information
    and truth, 15
    protected, 128
Inoue, Kazuhisa, 127
Input, and sensation/perception, 14
Insecurity, 49
Instincts, trusting, 33, 141
Insurance companies, 45
Issues, focus on certain aspects,
    19-20

J

Jackson, La Toya, 52
Jackson, Michael, 52
Jacobsen, Kristin, 100
James, William, on belief, 88
Japan
    medical profession in, 61
    misleading language in
        government, 127

ABOUT THE AUTHOR

Jonni Kincher received her education in psychology at California State University, San Bernardino. She now lives in Oregon.

Her interest in psychology began when she was in third grade, but there were not very many psychology books for children to read "back then." She made psychology available to young people by designing special courses in academic psychology for third grade through high school. Since these were the first courses to attempt teaching children psychology as an academic course, she had to create her own materials.

She began teaching *Psychology for Kids Playshops* in 1983. "Kids" from ages 8 to 17 have "played" and learned about the subject of psychology in the *Playshops*. The ideas and materials for her books were developed and tested in the *Playshops*.

Jonni Kincher is also the author of three other books from Free Spirit Publishing: *Dreams Can Help: A Journal Guide to Understanding Your Dreams and Making Them Work for You*, the award-winning *Psychology for Kids: 40 Fun Tests That Help You Learn about Yourself*, and *Psychology for Kids II: 40 Fun Experiments That Help You Learn about Others.*

Free Spirit Publishing specializes in SELF-HELP FOR KIDS® books, as well as products for parents, educators, and counselors. We offer fiction and nonfiction titles on topics that include self-esteem, stress management, school success, social action, gifted education, and learning differences.

For a free copy of our Parents' Choice approved catalog, write or call:

Free Spirit Publishing Inc.
400 First Avenue North, Suite 616
Minneapolis, MN 55401-1730
Toll-free (800) 735-7323, Local (612) 338-2068
Fax (612) 337-5050
E-mail Help4kids@freespirit.com